MW00809682

In the Beginning Were Stories, Not Texts

In the Beginning Were Stories, Not Texts

Story Theology

C. S. SONG

CASCADE *Books* · Eugene, Oregon

IN THE BEGINNING WERE STORIES, NOT TEXTS
Story Theology

Copyright © 2011 C. S. Song. All rights reserved. Except for brief quotations in
critical publications or reviews, no part of this book may be reproduced in any
manner without prior written permission from the publisher. Write: Permissions,
Wipf and Stock Publishers, 199 W. 8th Ave., Suite 3, Eugene, OR 97401.

Cascade Books
An Imprint of Wipf and Stock Publishers
199 W. 8th Ave., Suite 3
Eugene, OR 97401

www. wipfandstock.com

ISBN 13: 978-1-60899-704-6

Cataloging-in-Publication data:

Song, Choan-Seng, 1929–

    In the beginning were stories, not texts : story theology / C. S. Song.

    viii + 172 p. ; 23 cm. Including bibliographical references.

    ISBN 13: 978-1-60899-704-6

    1. Storytelling — Religious aspects — Christianity. I. Title.

BT78 .S658 2011

Manufactured in the U.S.A.

Contents

Preface

DOING CHRISTIAN THEOLOGY THROUGH stories has become a major trend in Christian theology today. This is the way it should be. After all, the Bible is a storybook. Take away stories, and is the Christian Bible still the Bible? Writers are storytellers. Painters are storytellers. Even scientists are learning to be storytellers. The strange thing is that Christian theology, while trying to serve the storybook called the Bible, has often been largely a theology of ideas and concepts. This non-biblical trend has to be reversed. That is why the book you hold in your hand and have begun to read is called *In the Beginning Were Stories, Not Texts*.

Does not creation consist of stories? Is not Exodus a collection of stories? Is not the rise to power of King David a story? Is not prophet after prophet in ancient Israel and Judah a storyteller? Is not Jesus the storyteller of storytellers? Did he sot speak of the reign of God in parables—which are stories?

I am grateful to friends and colleagues at Wipf and Stock for making this "story book" available to the reading public. May we all—people in the pew, students in theological classrooms, teachers who try to figure out mysteries of God in the universe and on our planet earth—learn to be storytellers.

C. S. Song
Taiwan
May 1, 2010, Labor Day

In the Beginning Were Stories, Not Texts

THE STORY TIME! AUSTRALIAN aborigines will say, "dream time." What a beautiful expression! Story is conceived in the womb of dreams, nurtured and developed in it. And when the womb cannot hold it any longer, it gives birth to it. As a baby arrives from the womb of its mother, a story, when it matures, is discharged from the womb of dreams to be told in the circles of children, men, and women. If it is a good story—good in the sense of compelling—it will be told from one generation to another generation.

JOSEPH'S DREAMS

The future is won by those who dare to dream and to tell their dreams in stories. The dreams of Joseph, one of the twelve sons of Jacob, at once comes to mind (Genesis 37). He has dreamed extraordinary dreams and, not being able to keep them to himself, he tells them to his brothers. "Listen to this dream that I dreamed," he begins. Whether he tells his dreams in innocence, in pride, or perhaps with humor, we can only guess. "There we were, binding sheaves in the field. Suddenly my sheaf rose and stood upright; then your sheaves gathered around it, and bowed to my sheaf" (37:6–7). His brothers are not amused, but their displeasure does not stop him, and he tells them another dream. "Look," he says, quite excited, "the sun, the moon, and eleven stars were bowing down to me" (37:9). This time even his father is offended. "What kind of dream is this that you have had?" Father Jacob, scarcely concealing his annoyance, rebukes him and says, "Shall we indeed come, I and your mother and your brothers, and bow to the ground before you?" (37:10).

According to the story told in the rest of the book of Genesis, this is what happened. His parents and brothers, forced by the severe famine, had to come for help to Joseph, who had, in the meantime, risen to become the most influential politician in Egypt, second only to the Pharaoh.

Story is dream and dream is story. The Australian aborigines are right. Story time is dreamtime. We can also reverse it and say that dreamtime is story time. The future belongs to those who dare to dream and strive to convert their dreams to stories, stories of struggle, stories of suffering, also stories of hope, faith, and compassion. Is it not true that almost all prophets in ancient Israel and Judah were dreamers—Isaiah, Jeremiah, and Ezekiel, to mention only three? At the critical juncture of their nation's history, they dreamed powerful dreams, fantastic dreams, out-of-this-world dreams, then proceeded to tell their people stories of their dreams. Isaiah, the prophet of Israel in the eighth century BCE, is a case in point. As he tells it: "In the year that King Uzziah died, I saw the Lord sitting on a throne, high and lofty, and the hem of his robe filled the temple. Seraphs were in attendance above him; each had six wings: with two they covered their feet, and with two they flew. And one called to another and said:

> Holy, holy, holy is the Lord of hosts;
> the whole earth is full of his glory.

And in his dream and vision he saw "the pivots on the thresholds shake at the voices of those who called, and the house filled with smoke" (Isa 6:1–5). As we know, that dream of Isaiah's epitomized the long struggle of his nation to survive in the harsh realities of geopolitics that were changing the face of the ancient Near Eastern world.

SURROUNDING AN EVENING FIRE

It is said that people without vision will perish. We can also say, people who stop dreaming and who have no stories to tell will perish. Stories are hatched in dreams and handed down from one generation to the next. A song from the Pacific puts it in this way:

> Surrounding an evening fire
> a group of children listen,
> they listen and listen to the words,
> the words of the old man.

This old man, he draws a story,
a story from the ashes,
together with the flickering fire.

This old man he weaves a story,
a story from the fire,
together with the rising smoke.
This old man, he plants a story,
a story of the past,
and he plants it calmly.
The story rises with the smoke
to plant itself in
winds that are green.[1]

There is, to use an expression in Chinese, "a picture in the poem and a poem in the picture" (*shi chong you hua, hua chong you shi*).

The poem, so simple and natural, paints a picture of an old man telling stories to the children surrounding him. It may be a village marketplace, a dusty roadside under an age-old banyan tree, or a beach at the seaside. "Winds that are green" are sending fresh cool air to the old man telling the story and the children listening intently to his story. What a rustic scene and a peaceful image! You can almost hear cicadas singing in the trees and insects buzzing in the bushes. The voice of the old man is soft and calm, but the children are ardent and eager. As the story slowly trudges along, the old story the old man plants in the hearts and minds of the children becomes a new story, the story of the past is transformed into a story of the present.

This is the magic of story, the magic that connects the old and the new, converts the past to the present. The story, the old man the storyteller and the children the listeners, these three, are woven together into an event occurring here and now. This seems to be what the poem is alluding to when it concludes by saying: "The story rises with the smoke to plant itself in winds that are green." This is a poem. This is a picture. And the poem and the picture weave a story.

What does "green" mean? It means young, new, blooming. It means a new generation of children. It means future generations of men and women. Is this not why we still read ancient stories from West and East, past and present, and do not cease to be fascinated by them? Above all, is this not why we continue to read the Bible, the book of the stories told

---

1. "This Old Man," in *Songs of the Pacific*, 16.

many, many centuries ago in far, far away lands, moved by them, inspired by them, and renewed by them? We love stories because God loves them. How can we not love stories when God loves them in the first place?

"I LOVE TO TELL THE STORY"

There is a hymn called "I Love to Tell the Story" in many Christian hymnals. Most of us are familiar with it. We are not only familiar with it, but love to sing it. The hymn goes like this:

> 1. I love to tell the story / of unseen things above,
> of Jesus and His glory, / of Jesus and His love.
> I love to tell the story, / because I know 'tis true;
> It satisfies my longings / as nothing else can do.
>
> 2. I love to tell the story; / more wonderful it seems
> than all the golden fancies / of all our golden dreams.
> I love to tell the story, / it did so much for me;
> and that is just the reason / I tell it now to thee.
>
> 3. I love to tell the story; / 'tis pleasant to repeat
> what seems, each time I tell it, / more wonderfully sweet.
> I love to tell the story, / for some have never heard
> the message of salvation / from God's own holy Word.
>
> 4. I love to tell the story; / for those who know it best
> seem hungering and thirsting / to hear it like the rest.
> And when, in scenes of glory, / I sing the new, new song,
> 'Twill be the old, old story / that I have loved so long.

Do you love to tell the story of Jesus? Do you love to listen to it? Do you love to tell the stories that fill the Bible? Do you love to listen to them? Do you love to tell the familiar stories and listen to not so familiar stories from your own land? Do you love to listen to mostly unfamiliar stories and sometimes familiar stories from foreign lands? Theology, however else you may have known it and practiced it, in the ultimate sense of that word, is story telling and story listening. Theology, however you may have understood it and spent many agonizing hours over it, above all things, is God telling stories through countless people in every land through the ages because God loves stories.

IN THE BEGINNING WERE STORIES

So in the beginning were stories. Life begins with story. The whole universe begins with story. And creation begins, not with a horrendous explosion called the big bang, but with an idyllic story of how God created it. The story of creation begins with God. "In the beginning when God created the heavens and the earth," so the first chapter of Genesis in the Hebrew Bible tells us, "the earth was a formless void and darkness covered the face of the deep, while a wind [spirit] from God swept over the face of the waters" (Gen 1:1–2). This is the story of creation our forebears in the land of the ancient Near East handed down from one generation to the next when they gazed at the immense mysterious sky above them and surveyed the endless desert land that stretched before them. Is it an unscientific account of how the universe came into being? Maybe. Is it an illusory tale of an irrational mind that has taken flight into the world of religious fantasy, the world that does not exist? Definitely not.

Creation is God's story. It is the story of God in charge of the vast universe, big bang or no big bang. It is an old story, as old as the beginning of creation itself, but it becomes a new story, a story of many people in many lands when it is told in different versions in an infinite variety of ways. When human beings are faced with turbulence in the voyage of life, confronted with the world in chaos, encountered tragedy in history, they return to the beginning for God's assurance. This is why that prophet in the land of captivity pleaded with his fellow captives to listen when he addressed them:

> Have you not known? Have you not heard?
> Has it not been told you from the beginning?
> Have you not understood from the foundation of the earth?
> It is he who sits above the circle of the earth . . .
> who stretches out the heavens like a curtain,
> and spreads them like a tent to live in;
> who brings princes to naught,
> and makes the rulers of the earth nothing. (Isa 40:21–23)

The prophet was referring to the story of creation his audience had perhaps dismissed as old, ancient, and outdated. But he invited them to listen to it again and again until it was transformed into a new story, until it became their own story, a story of hope and faith, a story of a new beginning of their life and history.

It is John, the author of the Gospel that bears his name, who has grasped the deep meaning of the creation story and converted it to the incarnation story. In words of incomparable profundity and beauty he declares:

> In the beginning was the Word, and the Word was with God, and the Word was God. He was in the beginning with God . . . (John 1:1)

"The Word" here is an event that happened and a story of that event told in the beginning. The statement is deeply theological, but difficult to grasp. If we read "Story" instead of "Word," it is still deeply theological but less difficult to grasp:

> In the beginning was the Story, and the Story was with God, and the Story was God. The Story was in the beginning with God . . .

"In the beginning" was not just God, but "Story was with God." The Story was not simply with God, "the Story was God." This sounds a little heady and clumsy, but is there a better way of saying God is the God of story, that story is the "essence" of God, that story is the "nature" of God? Jesus, to paraphrase the author of John's Gospel, is that "Story of God who became flesh and lived among us, and we have seen his glory, the glory as of a father's only son, full of grace and truth" (John 1:14).

Who says theology has to be ideas and concepts? Who has decided that theology has to be doctrines, axioms, propositions? Theology, if it has to do with God, must have to do with stories, since God is the God of stories, since "in the beginning was the Story, and the Story was with God, and the Story was God." That is why God cannot but love stories. For God not to love stories is to deny being God. God without stories is an empty God. God who has no story to tell is a God of no substance. Is theology still theology if it sets aside stories, stories of God turned into the story of Jesus and stories of us human beings, and stories of Jesus and stories of us human beings turned into God's stories?

There is what I call "healthy agnosticism" in some Eastern religions and philosophies. Many of us know these famous first lines of *Tao Te Ching* (Classic of the Way and Its Virtue) attributed to Lao Tzu, the ancient Chinese philosopher:

The Tao (Way) that can be told of is not the eternal Tao;
The name that can be named is not the eternal name.
The nameless is the origin of Heaven and Earth;
The Name is the mother of all things . . .[2]

The Tao, the Way, the One, the First Principle, or the Origin of all things between heaven and earth, whatever you may call it, plays tricks with us human beings and our language. As soon as we name IT, it is no longer IT. No sooner have we uttered a concept to define IT than IT eludes us and is no longer what we define IT to be.

There is also "healthy agnosticism" in the Apostle Paul. After agonizing over the convoluted relationships between Jews and Gentiles in the divine dispensation in the eleventh chapter of his Letter to the Romans, he finally has to say, not in exasperation, but in relief:

O the depth of the riches and wisdom and knowledge of God!
How unsearchable are his judgments and how inscrutable his ways. (Rom 11:33)

This is Paul at his best—Paul not as a pretentious theologian. He knows how to keep silent in the presence of the inscrutable God. Most theologians try to say too much about God, but at the end of the day God is not any less real to the men and women who cannot make heads or tails of theological abracadabra.

"ALL I CAN DO IS TO TELL THE STORY"

God is not concept; God is story. God is not idea; God is presence. God is not hypothesis; God is experience. God is not principle; God is life. What is the best way to gain access to this God? How do we become aware of the presence of this God with us? Surely not by means of concepts, ideas, hypotheses, or principles, but by means of the life we live, the experiences we go through, in a word, by means of the stories we weave, the stories we tell and share.

I remember a story that has left a deep impression on me. It is a Jewish story, the story told by people who have gone through the trials of life in their long history of adversity and affliction.

---

2. See this English rendering in *A Source Book in Chinese Philosophy*, 139.

When the great Rabbi Israel Baal Shem-Tov saw misfortune threatening the Jews it was his custom to go into a certain part of the forest to meditate. There he would light a fire, say a special prayer, and the miracle would be accomplished and the misfortune averted.

Later, when his disciple, the celebrated Magid of Mezritch, had occasion, for the same reason, to intercede with heaven, he would go to the same place in the forest and say: "Master of the Universe, listen! I do not know how to light the fire, but I am still able to say the prayer." And again the miracle would be accomplished.

Still later, Rabbi Moshe-Leib of Sassov, in order to save his people once more, would go into the forest and say: "I do not know how to light the fire, I do not know the prayer, but I know the place and this must be sufficient." It was sufficient and the miracle was accomplished.

Then it fell to Rabbi Israel of Rizhyn to overcome misfortune. Sitting in his armchair, his head in his hands, he spoke to God: "I am unable to light the fire and I do not know the prayer; I cannot even find the place in the forest. All I can do is to tell the story, and this must be sufficient."

And it was sufficient.[3]

This is a heartrending story, yet a marvelous story, a story just to the point of what we have been discussing. There will hardly be people, including you and me, who, although not Jewish, will not find this story resonating in their hearts and minds. They may grind their theological axes when they debate the concept of God, the doctrine of salvation, the meaning of the church, its sacraments, or speaking in tongues; they ought to be humbled when they are confronted by this God of stories.

"All I can do is to tell the story," says Rabbi Israel of Rizhyn. There is a faint echo of apologetic tone here, but the good Rabbi does not have to be apologetic at all. Is there anything you can do except to tell stories in times of helplessness? When you are at a loss as what to do, does not telling stories enable you to regain your faith and hope? In times of crisis, whether personal or national, does not sharing stories help you turn crisis into opportunity? History in story shows us the way. Humor in story gives us courage. Hope in story empowers us for the future. In

3. From Wiesel, *Gates of the Forest*.

the midst of darkness, a story becomes a light illuming our way. Does not the creation story in the Hebrew Bible begin with God bringing light into darkness? Does it not tell us how God creates order out of chaos?

If there is a beginning, there must be an ending, so they say. If this is true of all things, it must be true of story as well. But when it comes to story, beginning and ending become closely related. When a story seems to arrive at the end, that end becomes a beginning again. This is another wonder of story. Story not only creates a beginning in the very beginning, it also creates a beginning out of an end. A child seems to be aware of this wonder of story instinctively. When the story his/her parents are telling is about to come to an end, a child will plead with them for another story. Even after one story after another sends them to sleep, stories continue in their dreams, nurturing their imagination, fostering their curiosity. Did we not say that for the Australian aborigines story time is dreamtime? Story and dream—they together redeem our lives from spiritual stalemate and save our world from moral decay. This must be why Joel, the prophet in Judah, during the Persian period of Jewish history (539–331), tried to inspire his compatriots with these stirring words:

Then afterward

I (God) will pour out my spirit on all flesh;
your sons and your daughters shall prophesy,
your old men and women shall dream dreams
and your young men and women shall see visions.
Even on the male and female slaves,
in those days, I will pour out my spirit. (Joel 2:28–29)

God and human beings, young and old, get locked together in stories and dreams through God's Spirit. The Spirit of God that works in the human spirit enables human beings to dream dreams and tell stories. To be filled with the Spirit of God is to be able to tell stories and dream dreams, besides speaking in tongues. Furthermore, all people—women, men, and children, old and young—and not just a few, can be filled with the Spirit to tell stories and dream dreams.

This is why there are numerous myths, legends, folktales, stories of life, death and eternal life in all tribes and peoples all over the world, East and West, South and North. Show me a tribe, any tribe, that has no myth to tell. There is none. Name for me a people that has no folktales to narrate. There is none. And bring me a woman, a man, a child, who has no life story to share. Again there is none. Should there be a tribe, a nation, a person with no story to tell and no dream to dream, they would have to invent it. For no one could live without story, just as God without story is not the subject of our faith and theology.

Why is this so? The answer has to be that God is a Story-God, a God who, with the stories God tells through innumerable people throughout the ages, creates beginnings, a God who, with stories, converts ends to beginnings, a God who, with powerful stories, transforms death into life, a God who, with tender and compassionate stories, turns despair into hope. This is why the story of God through Jesus cannot end at Jesus' death on the cross. There must the story of the empty tomb. The story of the crucifixion must be converted to the story of the resurrection.

LIFE IS THE HEART OF STORY

What is then the main concern of the Story-God? And what is the heart of human stories? It is life! The creation story in the Hebrew Bible is the story of life: life of the universe, life of all things in the sky and on the earth, the life beyond the time-space frame of our existence. Do we not, in the creation story, hear God say: "Let the earth bring forth living creatures of every kind" (Gen 1:24)? Does not this same God also say: "Let us make humankind in our image, according to our likeness" (1:26)? In another creation story we read an account of how "God formed human beings from the dust of the ground and breathed into their nostrils the breath of life and they became living beings" (2:7). God's stories vibrate with life; that is why human stories can reverberate with life, life with its joys and sorrows, life with hopes and despairs, life with birth, old age, illness and death, and life, through these passages of life, on its way to eternal life.

Life is the perennial concern of humanity and it is around life that stories are told and retold—origin of life, passages of life, destiny of life, and immortality of life. For Maoris, the native people of New Zealand, life is also the heart of the story of the creation of human beings. It is reminiscent of the creation story in the Hebrew Bible. This is how the Maori story goes:

> Tane [the god] proceeded to the *puke* (*Mons veneris*) of Papa [the Earth] and there fashioned in human form a figure in the earth. His next task was to endow that figure with life, with human life, life as known to human beings . . . . Implanted in the lifeless

image were the *wairua* (spirit) and *manawa ora* (breath of life), obtained from Io, the Supreme Being. The breath of Tane was directed upon the image, and the warmth affected it. The figure absorbed life, a faint sigh was heard, the life spirit manifested itself, and Hine-ahu-one, the Earth Formed Maid, sneezed, opened her eyes, and rose—a woman.

Such was the Origin of Woman, formed from the substance of the Earth Mother, but animated by the divine Spirit that emanated from the Supreme Being, Io the great, Io of the Hidden Face, Io the Parent, and Io the Parentless.[4]

The similarity between this Maori story and the Genesis story is unmistakable. Except for the name of the deity and except for the creation of "woman" first instead of "man," there is the divine spirit, the earth, the breath of life. Even the way the lifeless figure formed from the earth is made into a living being by the divine spirit is strikingly similar. Stories do bring us together as vulnerable human beings living a transient life in a transient world, and not as invincible human beings armed with beliefs and convictions that assure them of an immortal life.

THERE ARE NO STORIES IN HELL

As we have mentioned, story can turn despair into hope, sorrow into joy, even death into life, and hell into paradise. For this reason we cannot think of a life without stories, a world without stories, the universe without stories, and God without stories.

Stories can turn Hell into Paradise! What does this mean in the first place? It means that there are no stories in Hell. That is why people, from ancient times to the present time, are afraid of Hell. This is true whether you are Buddhist, Hindu, Muslim, or Christian. Does not fear of Hell take up a large portion of religious literature in practically all religions? Most of these stories "make one's hair stand on end" (*mau gu shu ran* in Chinese), that is, make one shudder in fear. Listen to this Buddhist story of Hell:

The departed spirit cannot escape from being boiled in an iron pot. Once in Hell, the departed one may at times be thrown on a steep mountain of swords and shed much blood; at times he may suffer from the excruciating pain of a high mountain of spears piercing his breast. Sometimes he is run over by a flam-

4. This Maori creation story is to be found in Eliade, *From Primitives to Zen*, 130.

ing wagon wheel which bears the weight of many thousands of stones; and at other times he is made to sink into a bottomless river of ice. Sometimes he is forced to drink boiling water, or to swallow molten iron, or he is roasted in roaring flames. In these circumstances he can obtain nothing to drink, let alone even hear drink mentioned....Though he may raise desperate cries for help from Heaven, he finds no response and his chances for pardon decrease each night.... Once you fall into Hell, repentance is of no value. No matter how long you wait, even till the end of time, you will repeat your cries in vain.[5]

We cannot but be amazed by the fanciful imagination in this description of Hell. What a religious teaching such as this tries to do is to inculcate the fear of Hell in the believers and to exhort them to do good deeds in their lives.

This reminds us of Jesus' parable of the rich man and Lazarus (Luke 16:19–31). In that parable the rich man found himself in Hades (Hell) after he had died, where he was being tormented. Then he called out, "Father Abraham, have mercy on me, and send Lazarus to dip the tip of his finger and cool my tongue, for I am in agony in these flames" (16:24). This is the reply he got from Father Abraham: "Child . . . between you and us a great chasm has been fixed, so that those who might want to pass from here to you cannot do so, and no one can cross from there to us" (16:26). It seems that even Jesus is not entirely free from the popular belief in Hell. But Jesus, who told the parable, "descended to hell," according to the Apostles' Creed that finally became the creed of the Western church in about the year 700. What does this mean? We will come back to the question later.

Let us, then, look at how Dante (1265–1321)—said to be Italy's greatest poet and author of *The Divine Comedy*, an account of his imaginary journey through Hell, Purgatory and his final glimpse of Heaven—describes the unspeakable horror he encounters in Hell. Dante, led by his Guide, is struck with fear as he reads these words at the vestibule of Hell:[6]

> I AM THE WAY INTO THE CITY OF WOE.
> I AM THE WAY TO A FORSAKEN PEOPLE.
> I AM THE WAY INTO ETERNAL SORROW.
> (*The Inferno*, Canto III)

5. From *Kobodaishi zenshiu*, III, 347–55, in De Bary, *Buddhist Tradition*, 297.
6. All these stanzas are from *The Inferno*.

As his journey progresses, Dante witnesses horrible scenes in which those in Hell undergo painful torment. He tells what he with his mind's eye witnesses:

> Thus we descended the dark scarp of Hell
> to which all the evil of the Universe
> comes home at last, into the Fourth Great Circle
>
> and ledge of the abyss. O Holy Justice,
> who could relate the agonies I saw!
> What guilt is man that he can come to this? . . .
>
> Here too, I saw a nation of lost souls,
> . . . they strained their chests
> against enormous weights, and with mad howls . . .
> (Canto VII)
>
> There is in Hell a vast and sloping ground
> called Malebolge, a lost place of stone
> as black as the great cliff that seals it round . . .
>
> Below, on my right, and filling the first ditch
> along both banks, new souls in pain appeared,
> new torments, and new devils black as pitch.
>
> All of these sinners were naked; on our side
> of the middle they walked toward us; on the other,
> in our direction, but with swifter stride . . .
>
> We had already come to where the walk
> crosses the second bank, from which it lifts
> another arch, spanning from rock to rock.
>
> Here we heard people whine in the next chasm,
> and knock and thump themselves with open palms,
> and blubber through their snouts as if in a spasm.
>
> Streaming from that pit, a vapor rose
> over the banks, crusting them with a slime
> that sickened my eyes and hammered at my nose . . .
>
> Once there, I peered down; and I saw long lines
> of people in a river of excrement
> that seemed the overflow of the world's latrines . . .
> (Canto XVIII)

What poetic imagination! Lurking within it is a universal fear of human beings for divine punishment in Hell. And how have religions, almost without exception, used people's fear of Hell to manipulate them into submission!

Whether it is a Buddhist's frightening story of Hell, Jesus' sober parable of Hell, or Dante's lurid description of Hell, they tell us at least one thing, paraphrasing a Chinese idiom: Fear of Hell is "the same with everyone everywhere" (*ren tong zhi shin, sin tong zhi li*). This is another illustration of how stories can travel back and forth across cultural and religious borders and converge at the deepest level of human consciousness. It may be that stories of this kind, that is, stories of Hell, for example, proceed from the unconscious. Does this not tell us that story theology is a theological effort to engage us human beings and God at the place where human beings are most vulnerable, naked, and defenseless?

At any rate, there are no stories in Hell. What stories can these tormented souls in Hell tell? Pain numbs their sensibility to things beautiful. Torment deprives them of ability for that which is noble. Groaning renders them impotent for that which is good. And in the darkness of pain, how can they perceive the light of truth? And love? It does not exist in Hell, love as the fountainhead of stories, the fertile soil of stories, the womb of stories. Above all, time comes to a standstill in Hell. There is no day and night any longer; all is night. There are no more four seasons of spring, summer, autumn, and winter; all is bleak winter all the time. When time stops, story too stops. As love is the soul of story, so time is the fabric of story. Without love and without time, how could there be story in Hell? Those in Hell have no story to share. Eternal silence falls on Hell. That is why Dante, at the gates of Hell, has to read these words: "BEYOND TIME I STAND," and "ABANDON ALL HOPE YE WHO ENTER HERE."[7]

If love is the soul of story and time the fabric of it, then hope is its impetus. When you abandon hope, you die, not only physically but spiritually. When you give up hope, even if you continue your physical life, you are reduced to being "the living dead" and "a walking corpse." But how could human beings into whom God breathes the breath of life to enable them to become living beings be reduced to "the living dead" and "a walking corpse"? It must be for this reason that Jesus "descended

---

7. Dante, *Inferno*, Canto III.

to Hell," to enliven those in Hell with love, time, and hope, to make them become living beings again, to give them the ability to tell stories again.

GOD LOVES STORIES

Story is a primary word. It is the primary word of God. It is the first word God uttered: When God says, "Let there be light," and there was light (Gen 1:3). Since God uttered these first words, stories have continued to proceed from God, told and retold in human myths, legends, folktales, fairytales, in stories of the lives of millions upon millions of people who have walked the earth. Stories flow from parents to their eager children, from village elders to village men and women, from professional story-tellers to their listeners. All sorts of stories are told by poets, novelists, playwrights, artists, performers, and entertainers on the stage and on the movie screen.

Stories are even told by thinkers, philosophers, and theologians, if they do not belittle stories and regard stories beneath their professional dignity to handle. But to belittle stories is to belittle God. How could they belittle God when their business first and foremost has to do with God? How could they regard it beneath their professional dignity to handle stories when they have to deal with stories from human beings into whom God has breathed the breath of life? And how can they profess to love God and their fellow human beings if they do not also love their stories, since both God and their fellow human beings are story-makers?

No wonder Jesus loves stories, because he is keenly aware of the most fundamental fact that both God and his fellow human beings love stories. He teaches people in stories, and what he does turns into stories. His parables are in essence stories, brief and succinct in form, but long and deep in meaning. They are told in plain and common-place language, but provocative and soul-searching in their implication. Jesus proclaims the rule of God, the heart of his message and ministry, in parables and stories.

"With what can we compare the reign of God," he asks his audience, "or what parable will we use for it?" (Mark 4:30). For him this is not merely a rhetorical device used by many preachers and evangelists to heighten the expectation of their listeners. By asking the question, Jesus is genuinely looking for a parable, a story, which would move the heart of his audience with the good news of God's rule. It does not take long for him to come up with a story that parabolically illuminates for his audience what he means by the rule of God. "The rule of God," with his voice echoing in the air on the slope of a hill or on the shore by a lake, he proceeds to say, "is like a mustard seed, which, when sown upon the ground, is the smallest of all seeds on earth, yet when it is grown it grows up and becomes the greatest of all shrubs, and puts forth large branches, so that the birds of the air can make nests in its shade" (4:31–32).

Whether the mustard seed is the smallest of all seeds on earth, and whether it becomes the greatest of all shrubs when it grows up, is beside the point. The point is that the rule of God may be modest and insignificant in the beginning, but it will grow to be impressive and important in the end as dispossessed people find shelter under it. Jesus must have concluded his short but powerful parable by saying: You, each one of you, are the rule of God! Is this not in line with some of the things he said in what is called the "Sermon on the Mount"? He, for instance, intimates to his listeners that "blessed are you," each one of you, "who are poor, for yours is the rule of God" (Luke 6:20).

And there is the parable of the laborers in the vineyard" (Matt 20:1–15). This is a parable stretched into a story, no longer brief and compact as many other parables, nonetheless at once profoundly parabolic and strikingly pertinent to down-to-earth life situations. You may call it a parable-story and a story-parable. In a parable such as this, Jesus shows himself a master storyteller who combines deep theological insights with penetrating perceptiveness of the human mind and the human community.

Jesus begins the parable with these familiar words: "For the rule of God is like," making it clear from the outset that his message and ministry of God's rule is the key to understanding the parable he is going to tell in a story. The rule of God is the stage of this story-parable. Losing sight of it, you reduce the parable-story to nothing more than a political protest against the social conventions that spare no compassion and justice for the socially marginalized people. It must be for this reason that Jesus deliberately sets the climactic moment at the very end of the story-parable when all laborers, including those hired early in the morning and those hired almost at the end of the day, "received the [same] usual daily wage" (20:9).

The rule of God consists of stories such as this. Jesus does not confuse people with a theory of justice; he tells a story to bring home to them, literate and illiterate alike, the injustice prevailing in their society and the just society envisioned by him in God's rule. He does not force people to accept a concept of equality. What he does is to tell a story that encourages them not to acquiesce to the disparate and shameful way they are treated in society Instead, they are to stand to be counted for true equality, the cornerstone of God's rule. He does not baffle them with an abstract idea of human dignity. Instead, he implants in them a story, making them aware that their daily subsistence is essential to their dignity as human beings and that the rule of God is not rule *of God* if it does not assure them of their daily subsistence and of their dignity as human beings.

Who says God is silent? It is those who have no appreciation of stories that say God is silent. Who has postulated that God is mute? It is those who have no fascination for stories that have postulated that God is mute. There are people, even believers, who assert that they have not seen God, because they have not encountered God in stories. There are also men and women who look everywhere except in stories for the presence of God, but where else would they find God if not in stories of people who struggle to live in a harsh world and seek to live a meaningful life in a world beset with uncertainty, anxiety and fear?

Telling a story is then not a pastime, not something you do when you have nothing else to do. It is a serious business, because it is first God's business and then becomes our business. Listening to stories is not a waste of time. How can we be wasting our time when we listen to God's stories? If this is not the case, we have to say that prophets of ancient Israel wasted all their time listening to God. If this is not the case, we have to conclude that Jesus wasted his precious time at the critical moment of his life praying to God, saying: "Father, if you are willing, remove this cup from me; yet not my will but yours be done" (Luke 22:42). If this not the case, all Christian believers and believers of other faiths in the past and today have wasted their time praying to God and listening to what God has to say to them. And if this is not the case, our prayers are nothing but us talking to ourselves, or to use the Apostle Paul's words, we pray "as though beating the air" (1 Cor 9:26).

Telling stories and listening to them, then, is not an option; it is a necessity. It is not a choice, but an obligation. It is not something we can take or leave, but a matter of life or death. For in the beginning were stories, not texts.

2

Story Is the Matrix of Theology

THEOLOGY AND STORY ARE inseparable. Where there is story, there is theology. A story worthy of its name is a story that grips you in the depths of your heart and mind, forces you to look deeply into yourself and into human nature, and compels you to examine relations between you and other human beings, between human beings and the world, nature and creation, and relations between human beings and God. If this is what story does, it is already profoundly theological. It invites us to reflect on the roots of who we are and what we are, what the world around us is, and ultimately who and what God must be. Story is the matrix of theology.

THEOLOGY IN STORIES

Is then theology separable from story?· It can be. But it can do so only to its own detriment. If in the beginning was the story, if that story becomes translated into the story of Jesus for generations of Christians, into the history of the world and the lives of you and me, and most important of all, if God loves stories, it is inconceivable for theology to be theology when it keeps aloof from stories, and even worse, when it detaches itself from stories. I hope this is obvious from what we discussed in the previous chapter. For theology to be theology, it must be story theology.

It is evident that there are internal and inherent relationships between story and theology. Story contains within itself seeds of theology. It is the task of theology to identify theological seeds in stories, investigate the environments in which they grow, inquire ways in which they impact people and their surroundings as they grow. But the effort of theology does not stop here. It will develop, and draw implications from what they have perceived in stories and from ways in which stories are created and recreated, told and retold, in different settings and conditions, by different people in their different life situations.

You may then ask: what about the church? Is the church no longer important for theology? Did not Cyprian, bishop of Carthage, writing in 251, make the point of saying: "You cannot have God as father unless you have the Church as mother" (*Habere iam non potest Deum patrem qui ecclesiam qui non habet matrem*)?[1] Throughout the history of Christianity this view of the church has remained the basic article of faith for the church and Christians, whether Orthodox, Roman Catholic, or Protestant. As Christians we are familiar with the Apostles' Creed. It begins by stating: "I believe in God the Father Almighty, creator of heaven and earth," and concludes with these words towards the end: "I believe in the holy Catholic Church." But is it not belief in "the holy Catholic Church" that develops the belief in "God the Father almighty, created the Trinitarian doctrine of God, Son, and Spirit, and above all, defines the meaning of salvation? Some theologians today even assert that "the doctrine of the church has, in the last decade or so, moved to the forefront of theological research and writing, primarily among non-evangelicals—so much so that ecclesiology has effectively displaced the doctrine of revelation as 'first theology.'"[2]

This observation is not entirely true in Asia, for example, where Christianity in most of its nations is not a dominant force in society. One cannot but wonder also if it is quite true in Europe where the church, after having enjoyed privileges and power for centuries, suffers from both numerical decline and waning of influence outside the church. It may be that this is one of the reasons why some theologians seek to restore the doctrine of the church to the center of the Christian faith community, calling it "first theology."

I do not question the importance of the church for Christianity. Almost all religions rally around a community as the basis of their beliefs, rituals, and religious life. *Sangha* is one of the three jewels for Buddhism alongside the Buddha and *Dharma*. Family that constitutes the backbone of society is the heart of Confucian ethics, just to give a couple

---

1. See "Cyprian of Cathage on the Unity of the Church," in McGrath, *Christian Theology Reader*, 261–62.

2. So Vanhoozer, "Evangelicalism and the Church," 63.

of examples. What I am questioning is whether the importance of the church has overshadowed the importance of the Spirit and whether the Christian church is the sole custodian of God's truth for the theologians who emphasize ecclesiology as "the first theology." At least in Asia this is not the case as more theologians and thinking Christians have become aware of the "non-Christian" realities of the world in which they live, practice Christian faith and engage themselves in Christian theology.

Yes, there are stories in the church throughout its history in the West and in the East, and in the South as well as in the North. Where there is church, there are stories, stories of how people have come to believe in Jesus as their savior, stories of how many Christian believers have suffered persecution and martyrdom, stories of how churches are built in hostile situations, and stories of how the Christian community has grown in numbers and strength. The church has many stories to celebrate. These are stories of faith, hope and love, and therefore they are stories for theology.

TAKE IT AND READ

One of the most celebrated stories in the history of Christianity is that of the conversion of Augustine (354–430), later to become Bishop of Hippo in North Africa and to leave an indelible influence on the theology of the Latin Church in the centuries after him. Let him tells us the story himself:

> I probed the hidden depths of my soul and wrung its pitiful secrets from it, and when I mustered them all before the eyes of my heart, a great storm broke within me, brining me a great deluge of tears. . . . I flung myself down beneath a fig tree and gave way to the tears which now streamed from my eyes. . . . I had much to say to you, my God, not in these very words but in this strain: *Lord, will you never be content? Must we always taste your vengeance? Forget the long record of our sins.* For I felt that I was still the captive of my sins, and in my misery I kept crying "How long shall I go on saying 'tomorrow, tomorrow?' Why not now? Why not make an end of my ugly sins at this moment?"
>
> I was asking myself these questions, weeping all the while with the most bitter sorrow in my heart, when all at once I heard the sing-song voice of a child in a nearby house. Whether it was the voice of a boy or a girl I cannot say, but again and again it repeated the refrain "Take it and read, take it and read." At this

I looked up, thinking hard whether there was any kind of game in which children used to chant words like these, but I could not remember ever hearing them before. I stemmed the flood of tears and stood up, telling myself that this could only be a divine command to open my book of Scripture and read the first passage on which my eyes should fall . . .

So I hurried back to the place where Alypius was sitting, for when I stood up to move away I had put down the book containing Paul's Epistles. I seized it and opened it, and in silence I read the first passage on which my eyes fell: *Not in reveling and drunkenness, not in lust and wantonness, not in quarrels and rivalries. Rather, arm yourselves with the Lord Jesus Christ; spend no more thought on nature and nature's appetites* [Rom 14:1]. I have no wish to read more and no need to do so. For in an instant, as I came to the end of the sentence, it was as though the light of confidence flooded into my heart and all the darkness of doubt was dispelled . . .³

This is a classic conversion story, moving and dramatic. It is repeated again and again in the history of Christianity. It is told, with variations, by many women and men who experienced conversion. It is even to be found in the literature of other religions, understandably with much greater variations. As far as Augustine is concerned, how much his conversion story was to shape his Christian faith can be seen in his voluminous theological writings.

Augustine wrote *Confessions* "at the age of about 43, when he had become bishop of Hippo [covering] the first thirty-three years of his life."⁴ It is an autobiography written in the form of a prayer from beginning to end. In this long prayer and through it Augustine "gapes at mountain peaks, at the boundless tides of the sea, the broad sweep of rivers, the encircling ocean and the motions of the stars."⁵ He sums up his deep spiritual experience of God in these unforgettable words at the very outset of *Confessions*: "you (God) made us for yourself and our hearts find no peace until they rest in you."⁶ This is the heart of the story of his life to which he gave an eloquent and moving account in his *Confessions*. His voluminous theological writings that preceded his conversion expe-

---

3. See Augustine *Confessions* 8.12, 177–78.

4. Brown, *Augustine of Hippo*, 28.

5. Augustine *Confessions* 10.13, 15. See Brown, *Augustine of Hippo*, 168.

6. Augustine *Confessions* 1.1.

rience and his theology that followed it should be comprehended and appreciated in the light of this story of his life. In the *Confessions*, it is pointed out, Augustine "invited his readers to place his theology in the context of his experience, as he did."[7]

Just as an example of how his life story gets reflected in his theological writings we may refer to *The City of God*, his monumental theology of history. Augustine began to write *The City of God* when Rome was sacked by Alaric the Goth in 410, "the event that gave the ancient world the shock (caused by) by the fall of the Roman Empire."[8] In it we find these words:

> Accordingly, two cities have been formed by two loves: the earthly by the love of self, even to the contempt of God; the heavenly by the love of God, even to the contempt of self. The former, in a word, glories in itself, the latter in the Lord. For the one seeks glory from men; but the greatest glory of the other is God, the witness of conscience. The one lifts up its head in its own glory; the other says to its God, "Thou art my glory, and the lifter of mine head." In the one, the princes and the nations it subdues are ruled by the love of ruling; in the other, the princes and the subjects serve one another in love, the latter obeying, while the former take thought for all. The one delights in its own strength, represented in the persons of its rulers; the other says to its God, "I will love Thee, O Lord, my strength." And therefore the wise men of the one city, living according to man, have sought for profit to their own bodies or souls, or both . . . . But in the other city there is no human wisdom, but only godliness, which offers due worship to the true God, and looks for its reward in the society of the saints, of the holy angels as well as holy men, "that God may be all in all."[9]

The contrast Augustine draws between the earthly city that is Rome and the heavenly that is the city of God cannot be sharper.

The language here is very personal, the imageries are very vivid, and the portrayal of the two cities is not so much historical as spiritual. One recalls these words of Augustine's towards end of his *Confessions*:

> I have learnt to love you late [O Lord], Beauty at once so ancient and so new! I have learnt to love you late! You were within me,

---

7. Miles, *Word Made Flesh*, 95.

8. See Batternhouse, *Companion to the Study of St. Augustine*, 259.

9. Augustine *City of God* 14.28, 477.

and I was in the world outside myself. I searched for you outside myself and, disfigured as I was, I fell upon the lovely things of your creation. You were with me, but I was not with you. The beautiful things of this world kept me far from you and yet, if they had been in you, they would have had no being at all . . .[10]

How the story of his life intertwined with his theology that explores the love and hate relationships between the city of God and the city that is Rome! In a true sense, Augustine's theology is the theology of the story of his life. Should this not also be true for most theologians and thinkers?

In volume after volume of Augustine's theological writings, we perceive the story of two men struggling

> like Esau and Jacob in the womb of Rebecca. . . . There was . . . the man of the world, the developed humanist with enough tincture of Platonism to gild the humanism; and there was the Augustine of the "Confessions," of the "Sermons," of the "De Civitate," the monk, the ascetic, the other-worldly preacher, the biblical expositor, the mortified priest.[11]

Does this not tell us that stories, personal, familial, societal, national, are the matrix of theology? Is not theology generated out of the interactions of these stories with the story of God the creator and redeemer?

Another example is Augustine's treatment of the doctrine of the Trinity in his treatise that "ranks as one of his foremost works, and indeed as one of the ablest presentations of the doctrine in Christian literature."[12] How does Augustine approach this most fundamental and yet most difficult subject of Christian faith that, in his own words, "in no other subject is error more dangerous, or inquiry more laborious, or discovery of truth more profitable"?[13] It is not from the height of his theological reason but from the depth of his human experience that he tried to penetrate the mystery of the triune God.

Particularly from the human experience of memory! What is memory if not stories of life and faith? What is theology if not explora-

---

10. Augustine *Confessions* 10.27.

11. Figgis, *Political Aspects*, 114, quoted by Edward R. Hardy Jr., "The City of God," in Battenhouse, *Companion to the Study of St. Augustine*, 280.

12. Cyril C. Richardson, "The Enigma of the Trinity," in Battenhouse, *Companion to the Study of St. Augustine*, 235.

13. Augustine *De Trinitatis* 1.2.5. Quoted by Richardson in Battenshouse, *Companion to the Study of St. Augustine*, 235.

tion of memory in which God and human being are locked in efforts to fathom the meaning of life present and eternal? Augustine must have realized the memory that stores the stories of life and faith is the matrix of theology, even for an abstruse topic such as the Trinity. It must be for this reason that he devotes much space to reflecting on memory in his *Confessions*, the story of his life and faith. In the *Confessions* he prays to God, hardly able to conceal his wonder for memory:

> The power of the memory is prodigious, my God. It is a vast, immeasurable sanctuary. Who can plumb its depths? And yet it is a faculty of my soul. Although it is part of my nature, I cannot understand all that I am. It means, then, that the mind is too narrow to contain itself entirely.[14]

What is theology if not to fathom deeply this prodigious memory, this vast storage of stories of life and faith? It is in and through his memory, his stories of life and faith, that Augustine engages himself in theology. In his own words in the *Confessions*:

> See how I have explored the vast field of my memory in search of you, O Lord! And I have not found you outside it. For I have discovered nothing about you except what I have remembered since the time when I first learned about you. Ever since I have not forgotten about you . . . . you have always been present in my memory, and it is there that I find you. . . .[15]

Were more theologians as candid as Augustine in his *Confessions*, giving a more prominent place to their memory, stories of their life and faith!

Augustine makes no secret of his own experience as he explores the most fundamental and yet most difficult topic of the Trinity. This is what he tells us, among other things:

> For I remember I have memory, will, and understanding; and I understand that I understand and will and remember; and I will that I will and remember and understand; and I remember together my whole memory and understanding and will.[16]

A little convoluted, no doubt. What does this have to do with Augustine's treatment of the topic of the Trinity? "Considering and rejecting many

14. Augustine *Confessions* 10.8.

15. Ibid., 10.24.

16. Augustine *De Trinitatis* 10.11.18; quoted by Richardson in Battenhose, *Companion to the Study of St. Augustine*, 250.

possible explanations, he finally isolated a model for the internal relationships of the Trinity in the human functions of memory, understanding, and will."[17]

Is it, then, not true to say that in writing the *Confessions*, the story
of his life and faith, in his mid-life, Augustine provided us with a key to
his prolific theological writings, including *The City of God* and *On the
Trinity*?

"Where is the water you are going to bring to me?"

There are of course stories outside Christianity, more stories than you
can find in the Christian church, as a matter of fact, for the simple reason
that there are more people outside the Christian church than inside it, at
least two-thirds of the world population. These stories are equally rich
in theological meanings, since they are stories of how people struggle
for faith, hope and love in the midst of fear, pain and suffering. If they
are stories of faith, hope and love, are they not also legitimate sources
of Christian theology? They are first Buddhist stories, Hindu stories,
Muslim stories, Jewish stories, Confucian stories, or stories of primal
religions. But can they not also be "Christian" stories if we believe that
in the beginning was the Story, the Story of God, maker of heaven and
earth? Similarly, Christian stories of faith, hope and love can be stories
for Zen Buddhists, Taoists, Hindus, Sikhs, or Muslims. In actual fact,
do not Judaism, Christianity and Islam have a great deal in common in
scriptures and histories?

The question for us is then: How do stories, Christian stories and
other stories, interact with theology, in our case, Christian theology?
This will be the main concern that will engage us in the following
chapters of this book. But before proceeding any further, let us listen
to a Hindu story and see if we as Christians can hear our echoes of life
and faith in it.

> A famous ascetic named Narada, having obtained the grace of
> Vishnu by his numberless austerities, the god appears to him
> and promises to do for him anything he may wish. "Show me
> the magical power of thy Maya," Narada requests of him. Vishnu
> consents, and gives the sign to follow him. Presently they find
> themselves upon a desert road in hot summer, and Vishnu, feel-

---

17. Miles, *Word Made Flesh*, 108.

ing thirsty, asks Narada to go on a few hundred yards farther where there is a little village, and fetch him some water.

Narada hastens forward and knocks at the door of the first house he comes to. A very beautiful girl opens the door; the ascetic gazes upon her at length and forgets why he has come. He enters the house, and the parents of the girl receive him with the respect due to a saint. Time passes, Narada marries the girl, and learns to know the joy of marriage and the hardships of a peasant life. Twelve years go by. Narada has now three children and, after his father-in-law's death, becomes the owner of the farm.

But in the course of the twelfth year, torrential rains inundated the region. In one night the cattle are drowned and the house collapses. Supporting his wife with one hand, holding two of his children with the other and carrying the smallest on his shoulder, Narada struggles through the waters. But the burden is too great for him. He slips and the little one falls into the water. Narada lets go of the other two children to recover him, but too late, the torrent has carried him far away. Whilst he is looking for the little one, the waters engulf the two others and, shortly afterwards, his wife. Narada himself falls, and the flood bears him away unconscious, like a log of wood. When, stranded on a rock, he comes to himself and remembers his misfortunes, he bursts into tears.

But suddenly he hears a familiar voice: "My child! Where is the water you were going to bring me? I have been waiting for you more than half an hour!" Narada turns his head and looks. Instead of the all destroying flood, he sees the desert landscape dazzling in the sunlight. And the god asks: "Now do you understand the secret of my maya?"[18]

There is a lot of theology in this story, theology in the sense of interactions between the divine and the human in the recesses of the human heart and in the depths of human community.

Twelve Years or Half an Hour?

This Hindu story contains a subtle theology of time. For Narada it has been twelve long years, but for Vishnu the god it is a mere half an hour! What makes us pause in this story is not the quantitative difference between twelve years and half an hour, but the qualitative difference between Narada's time and Vishnu's time, infinite distinctness between human time and divine time. Our time, whether it is an hour, twenty-

---

18. The story is to be found in Eliade, *Images and Symbols*.

four hours, even a hundred years, is for God a mere half an hour, a few minutes, a fraction of a second, even no time at all.

The story reminds one of the Buddhist concept of *kalpa* (*chieh* in Chinese). Kalpa means "a fabulous period of time, a day of Brahma or 1,000 Yugas, a period of four hundred and thirty-two million years of mortals, measuring the duration of the world."[19] This is an astonishing quantity of time, meaning that Kalpa is an infinite duration of time. It is "an *aeon* of incalculable time."[20]

The term *kalpa* may sound unfamiliar to Christians, but the term *aeon* is familiar to them. It is a biblical term and a Christian theological concept. The term is "used in the Septuagint [the LXX, a translation of the Hebrew Scripture made in the middle of the second century BCE] and in the New Testament in the sense of 'long span of time,' 'eternity.' After the first century BCE, it becomes, in the meaning of 'world's age' and 'world,' the term for the apocalyptic doctrine of the present and the coming *aeon*."[21]

Whether it is the Hindu *kalpa*, the Buddhist *kalpa*, or the Christian *aeon*, time stretches human imagination to a breaking point until it breaks down, forcing human beings to take flight into the eternity that supersedes time, into the apocalyptic world of joy and fulfillment that transcends the present world of pain and suffering. In the story of Vishnu and Narada, no such metaphysical terms as *kalpa* and *aeon* are used. It simply refers to the twelve years of Narada and Vishnu's half an hour, the periods of time from our everyday life. And yet, these everyday-life words obscure the meaning of time incalculable in our experience of time. What one has to do is to resort to an apocalyptic language, the language of visions, images and symbols. In the apocalyptic language religions encounter one another in the presence of eternity. And it is a story such as Narada and Vishnu that leads its readers into time beyond time, even time beyond eternity. What is this time beyond time? What is this time beyond eternity? Here the story of Vishnu and Narada reverts

19. See Soothhill and Hodus, *Dictionary of Chinese Buddhist Terms*, 232a. It is further pointed out that ". . . a month of Brahma is supposed to contain thirty such kalpas; according to the Mahabharata twelve months of Brahma constitute his year, and one hundred such years his lifetime; fifty years of Brahma are supposed to have elapsed . . ."

20. Ibid., 232a.

21. See Buttrick, *Interpreter' Dictionary of the Bible*, 52b.

back to the mundane time of twelve years and half an hour, enabling the reader to experience that incalculable time of eternity.

Is this not an example of the story of time being the matrix of the theology of time?

"Show me the magical power of Maya"

Maya is a Sanskrit word for delusion or illusion; the Chinese equivalent is *mi*, meaning delusion, illusion *and* confusion. *Maya* is the world of delusion, illusion and confusion; it is the world in which the unreal is taken for the real, the false for the true, evil for good. It is the upside-down world from which one has to be set free.

Narada has worked very hard to set himself free from the world of *maya* "through numberless austerities," the story tells us. The story, in these few words, portrays an ascetic who has attained "the perfection of wisdom" epitomized in the Buddhist *Heart Sutra*: "form is emptiness, and the very emptiness is form; emptiness does not differ from form, form does not differ from emptiness; whatever is form, that is empti-ness, whatever is emptiness, that is form. The same is true of feelings, perceptions, impulses, and consciousness."[22] Do not these words echo quite unmistakably the opening words of Ecclesiastes in the Hebrew Bible that say: "Vanity of vanities! All is vanity" (1:2)?

The language of emptiness in the Buddhist *Heart Sutra* and that of vanity in Ecclesiastes are all abstract, sounding very "religious," but exerting no real impact on the life people live. But these "abstract" concepts did not generate of themselves; they are acquired after a long experience of life in the world of vanity and emptiness. The story of Narada and Vishnu compels us to sit back and reflect on the meaning of *maya* in a way no abstract concept of emptiness could ever do.

Despite his efforts to attain the truth about *maya* after many years of asceticism, Narada falls right into it when the first opportunity offers itself. He forgets the god Vishnu's request to bring water, gets happily married, to be followed by the fierce torrential rains in which he had lost his wife, children and everything. We then find Narada stranded on a rock, bursting into tears. Here again the story of Narada becomes the matrix of reflections on the world as delusion, illusion and confusion.

22. This is how the Buddhist Scripture of *The Heart Sutra* begins (see Conze, *Buddhist Scriptures*, 162–63).

"Now you have understood the Secret of Maya"

The strenuous ascetic efforts and silent meditations have not revealed to Narada the secret of Maya, but happiness and sorrow in the world have! This is what the story conveys to its readers. The tragic happenings caused by the devastating storm depicting a desperate man trying to save the happiness he has accumulated for twelve years in the midst of the raging deluge are all too vivid, intense and real. If it happens to the ascetic Narada, it can also happen to all of us.

Religious books filled with instructions of how to be free from *maya*, spiritual exercises of meditation to contemplate the futility of *maya*, or theological discourse on the vanity of the world in which we live, are no match for a story such as this that recounts the miseries of life in the fleeting world of illusion. Story has the power to grip its readers to the core of their being, shaking them out of their complacency about themselves, wake them up from their transient life and the world of uncertainty.

Let us read once again the tragic scene so plainly and yet so graphically described in the story. Engulfed in the merciless deluge, Narada,

> supporting his wife with one hand, holding two of his children with the other and carrying the smallest on his shoulder, struggles through the waters. But the burden is too great for him. He slips and the little one falls into the water. Narada lets go of the other two children to recover him, but too late, the torrent carried him far away. Whilst he is looking for the little one, the waters engulf the two others and, shortly afterwards, his wife. Narada himself falls and the flood bears him away unconscious, like a log of wood. When, stranded on a rock, he comes to himself and remembers his misfortunes, he bursts into tears.

The story is told in the present tense, which adds to the realism described in unsophisticated plain language. Who is Narada? He is not just a Hindu ascetic unrelated to us; Narada is you and me. Who is Narada? He is not merely someone in the past; he is us, all of us, past, present, and future, who walk the earth. The story is the story of us all in the grip of *maya*, yet not realizing it. How many times in the course of life you and I have to find ourselves stranded on a rock, remembering our miseries and bursting into tears!

"My child, where is the water you were going to bring me?"

The Hindu story may be a vivid description of the illusion of life and world, some of us may concede, but does it have any redemptive meaning? Redemption is the question Christians are always ready to direct to non-Christian stories such as this Hindu story. But when we read the story not encumbered by traditional teachings of the church and a Christian theological definition of redemption, we can clearly perceive the power of redemption at work in this Hindu story.

As Narada is in utter despair, he hears the god Vishnu ask him: "My child, where is the water you were going to bring me?" The voice is gentle and not harsh; it is compassionate and not indignant. My child! Narada is still his child, even though Narada has forgotten to bring him water. Narada has not ceased to be his child, even though Narada allows himself to stray into the world of *maya* despite years of ascetic efforts.

This does remind us of Jesus' parable of "the father's love," commonly known as the parable of the prodigal son (Luke 15:11–32). At the end of this heightened drama the father says to the disgruntled elder son: "But we had to celebrate and rejoice, because this brother of yours was dead and has come to life; he was lost and has been found" (15:32). Is not Narada lost but found again by Vishnu, the god?

Is not this Hindu story the matrix of Hindu theology of redemption, even Christian theology of redemption?

A MAN BORN BLIND

John, the author of the Gospel that bears his name, is a brilliant theologian and also a magnificent storyteller. Perhaps he is a storyteller first, then a theologian. To put it differently, it is from stories, real-life stories, that his theology has developed and grown. Take that abstruse theological statement immortalized in Christian faith and theology. I am referring to the opening words in the prologue to his Gospel.

> In the beginning was the Word, and the Word was with God, and the Word was God. All things came into being through him, and without him not one thing came into being. What has come into being in him was life, and the life was the light of all people. The light shines in darkness, and the darkness did not overcome it. (John 1:1–5)

This is a very abstruse statement. Who can understand it? Did John, the author of the Gospel, understand what he was saying? If he did, how did he understand it? By sudden revelation from above, or through the stories he lived and experienced as a believer and evangelist? It must be the latter. He was a storyteller first, then a theologian. This is evident in the story he told about the man born blind (John 9). It is a long story. Why did John take his time to tell such a long story? It must be because he sees in the story a host of theological insights!

It is a dramatic story. It is a life drama that involves many actors: the blind man himself, his parents, the religious authorities, and above all Jesus. His profound theological statement in the prologue must have grown out of stories such as the story of the man born blind, a story he told so dramatically and almost breathtakingly.

"Rabbi, who sinned?"

As the story begins, Jesus is the first to appear on the stage. The story of the man born blind John the author is about to tell is in fact a Jesus-story. It is Jesus who makes the story happen. It is Jesus who is the center of the drama. And it is Jesus who commands the attention from beginning to end. Then, only then, the man born blind appears on the scene.

But even after the man born blind has appeared on the scene, it is not his physical condition that is the issue; it is the question of sin, or more precisely, the question of who sinned, causing the man to be born blind: the man himself? his parents? or his ancestors? This is a theological question that preoccupies his disciples. It is a theological question that demands a theological answer. For the disciples the question of who sinned is more important that the man who lost his eyesight when he was born.

It is not surprising that people of olden days who associated illness with sin regarded physical impediment as a religious matter; even today many religious believers think the same way. That is why temples and shrines are filled with faithful devotees praying to their gods to rid them of their bad *karma* and heal their illnesses. Is this not also what many devout Christians do when they worship God and pray to God?

This reminds me of one of my former students in Taiwan who was hospitalized for a serious illness. I visited him in the hospital. He was in pain and barely able to speak. As soon as he saw me, he looked at me with teary eyes, mustering whatever strength he had, and asked me:

"What sin have I committed to deserve such punishment from God?" If even someone like him with a theology degree believes that illness is divine punishment, how much more those Christian men and women who have not gone through theological training!

"Neither this man nor his parents sinned"

As to Jesus, his answer to the disciples is blunt. Without mincing his words, he says to them: "Neither this man nor his parents sinned." With a stroke of theological boldness he dismissed the time-honored belief that illness is caused by one's own sin or by the sin inherited from one's parents.

This is another moment of theological truth that John highlights in the story of the man born blind. He does not have Jesus engage with the disciples to refute the teachings of his religious tradition. Nor does he have Jesus develop a set of teachings arguing that illness has nothing to do with sin, hereditary or not. It is not doctrine but a man born blind, a man who has suffered all his life because of his blindness, a man despised by others because he could not see, that Jesus has to deal with. The man born blind is not a doctrine, nor is he a teaching. He is a story, a story of pain and suffering, a story of indignity and humiliation. He is a story of life, a life of pain, agony, and suffering. This story is full of theological lessons, particularly the lesson that theology has to be deeply rooted in the story of interactions between the compassionate God and the suffering human being.

Is this not the reason why Jesus declares to the disciples, to the men and women waiting anxiously for what is going to happen next, and to the man born blind: "He was born blind so that God's works might be revealed in him"? Revealing God's works in the man born blind! What is it? Is it a miraculous healing? Is this what John, the storyteller-theologian, tries to prove in the story? Not likely. He goes to great lengths to show how Jesus went about bringing sight back to the man. He "spat on the ground and made mud with the saliva and spread the mud on the man's eyes" (9:6) and instructed him "to go and wash in the pool of Siloam" (9:7). This is not an instant healing. On the contrary, John seems at pains to show that the healing takes place as the result of elaborate medical procedure. Healing is a process, a biological and medical process. It at the same time is a spiritual process. Healing is a matter of mind and body. Is this not what John means by "God's work" in this healing story? We must note that in the story the word "miracle" is not used.

"Lord, I believe"

Nor does John have the man, whose sight has been restored by Jesus, say that what has happened to him is what is called "faith healing." In the story it is Jesus who, in response to the disciples' question about sin and illness, takes the initiative to heal the man, and not in response to the faith exhibited by him. His faith is not mentioned as a decisive factor in this healing story. Here John, the storyteller, is not telling a story of a faith healing. In fact the man's faith in Jesus is born only after he has been interrogated by the religious authorities and commanded by them to renounce Jesus as the healer. He has to say to them loud and clear: "I do not know whether he [Jesus] is a sinner. One thing I do know, that though I was blind, now I see" (9:25). This is a simple faith generated in a simple man who had gone through a life of pain and suffering because of his blindness. But his simple faith, his matter-of-fact faith, developed into a profound awareness of the love of God working through Jesus. He testifies to the religious authorities and says: "If this man [Jesus] were not from God, he could do nothing" (9:33)! This is the theological insight that penetrates the whole story. The story is the unfolding of this insight step by step, finally leading to the man's confession to Jesus: "Lord, I believe" (9:38).

From the man born blind to the disciples' question about sin and illness, to Jesus restoring sight to him, to his spirited arguments with the religious authorities, to his confession of Jesus as Lord—what a wealth of theological insights embedded in this story! For John, the author of the Fourth Gospel, story is "the matrix of theology." Theology is not concocted in the minds of theologians or manufactured in their study. It is unfolded from one stage to the next in the stories of men, women and children in their lives of doubt, pain and suffering, and in their experiences of hope against hope, in their faith in life despite the reality of death. Can you do theology apart from such stories? I hope you cannot. John, cannot do theology apart from stories. That is why he is such a fascinating theologian, and a profound one at that.

3

Theology Rewrites Stories

IN STORY WE ARE not just dealing with a "mere" story. This is evident from our discussion in the previous chapter. A story that holds theological seeds within itself cannot be a "mere" story. It can be a healing story bringing faith, hope and love to those in distress. At the same time it can be a dangerous story, dangerous to those who wield power over others. That is why there are always attempts to interfere with a dangerous story either to neutralize it or to rewrite it.

If human beings love stories and cannot do without them, they also have a penchant for rewriting stories, particularly the stories that contradict their interest and question their power and privilege. For this reason we, in spite of our fascination with stories as the primary source of our life, faith and theology, cannot take story, any story, at face value. The question as to who tells the story and retells it, who writes the story and rewrites it, becomes a very critical issue.

"THE VAIN CROW"

Those who hold power over others not only rewrite a story to suit their interest and purpose, but do not hesitate to exterminate those who write and tell stories to bear witness to the truth of the matter. Aesop, the famed storyteller of animal fables in sixth-century BCE Greece, is a prominent example. He was a slave but a person of wisdom and wit. After gaining his freedom, he "traveled to Athens, where he became a defender of the common people, using his fables to expose the unjust ways of tyrants." As was expected, he met his tragic end at the hand of a despotic ruler. "In 560 [BCE] Aesop was condemned to death . . . and was thrown over a cliff at Hypania."[1]

One of some two hundred fables ascribed to Aesop is a fable called "The Vain Crow." As the fable goes:

> A crow, as vain and conceited as only a crow can be, picked up the feathers that some peacocks had shed and stuck them among his own. Then he scoffed at his old companions and joined a flock of beautiful peacocks. After introducing himself with great self-confidence, the crow was immediately recognized for the intruder he was, and the peacocks stripped him of this borrowed plumes. Moreover, they battered him with their beaks and sent him about his business. The unlucky crow, sorely punished and deeply regretful, rejoined his former companions and wanted to mix with them again as if nothing had happened. But they recalled the airs he had assumed and drove him from their flock. At the same time, one of the crows whom he had recently snubbed gave him this short lecture: "Had you been satisfied with your own feathers, you would have escaped the punishment of your betters, and also the contempt of your equals."[2]

The crow is the main character in this fable. What does it represent? Who is supposed to be the crow? To whom does it point?

Aesop the storyteller knows what the crow represents, who it points to, and who it is supposed to be. His audience too knows what the crow represents, who it points to, who it is supposed to be. Both Aesop the storyteller and his audience are "aware of it without speaking out" (*shin li you shu*), to use a Chinese expression. Why are they so cautious? Because it is a matter of life and death for them. Once they speak what is on their minds, their lives would be in danger. The most people could do is what a Chinese idiom calls, *shin chao pu shiuan*, that is, "a tacit understanding or agreement" with what Aesop is telling them.

Not only Aesop the storyteller and the audience know what the crow refers to; there is someone else who also knows it. It is the ruler who rules them with an iron fist. Most likely, that ruler is a despot feared by his people, a dictator who has no compunction of torturing and murdering those who oppose him. When the fable reaches his ears, he is enraged. He has been furious about the ways in which Aesop the storyteller satirizes him by telling clever fables and inciting people against

---

1. See Zipes, "Introduction" to *Aesop's Fables*.

2. *Aesop's Fables*, 17.

him. And this fable is the last straw. He knows that the vain crow in the fable clearly refers to him. He is that ugly crow that joins the flock of beautiful peacocks. That makes him look even uglier and more ridiculous. Just as the peacocks regard the crow as an intruder, he is also regarded by his people as an intruder. He knows people are laughing at him behind his back. They do not consider him to be one of them. They would overthrow him if they could, pack him up and send him running, just as the peacocks have done with the crow.

How much the hated ruler wants to rewrite the fable! He has the power to do so, and there are always some people who are willing to do his bidding. But the story has gotten so popular that any attempt to tamper with it would make him more hated and look more ridiculous. What he could do is to do away with the author of the fable. That's exactly what he has done. He puts Aesop, the ingenious author of fables, to death. But the fact is that although he may be able to do away with Aesop, he is not able to do away with his fables. His fables have survived for more than two thousand years. His ingenious fables are alive and well even today, not only entertaining people who listen to them but providing courage and hope to men and women living under dictatorial rule.

"THE RAPE OF NANKING"

Throughout history, how common the impulse of those in power is to rewrite a story unfavorable to them! How they change a story to fit their purpose! It does make you wonder whether you can trust official historiography. How can you expect to know what has really happened if you rely entirely on the official account of it? Can you trust the history written by the historian serving at the pleasure of a totalitarian ruler and doing his bidding? That is why ancient Greece needed an Aesop to create fables, ancient China needed Confucius to write *Spring and Autumn Annals* based on the annals of the state of Lu (722–481 BCE) so that "rebellious ministers and villainous sons were struck with terror,"[3] or ancient Israel needed prophets such as Nathan to tell King David a story of the poor man's lamb and reprimand him for shamelessly committing adultery with the wife of his general and risking his life on the battlefield (2 Sam 12:1–15).

---

3. *The Works of Mencius*, Tang Wan Kung, Part II. In Legge, *Chinese Classics*, 283.

There are neo-Nazis in Germany who try to deny the Holocaust committed by the Nazi regime during World War II in Europe. That is why Elie Wiesel, the Holocaust survivor, breaks his silence to tell in story after story the atrocities committed against Jews, including his own father, in the German concentration camps and in the gas chambers. After the war the German government officially apologized to the Holocaust victims and survivors and "has paid at least DM 88 billion in compensation and reparations and will pay another DM 20 billion by the year 2005. If one factors in all the money the Germans have paid in compensation to individual victims, restitution for lost property, compensatory pensions, payments based on state regulations, final restitution in special cases, and money for global agreements with Israel and sixteen other nations for war damages, the total comes to almost DM 124 billion, or almost $60 billion."[4]

This is not to say that what the German government has done could compensate for the heinous crime the Nazi regime committed. No amount of money paid to the Holocaust survivors could bring the Holocaust victims back to life, nor could it heal the broken hearts of the victims' families. What is done cannot be undone. But at least the German government did what they could to atone for the crimes committed by the Nazi government.

When it comes to Japan, it is quite a different story. "The Japanese," it is pointed out, "have paid close to nothing for their war crimes." Not only this, "many leading officials in Japan continue to believe (or pretend to believe) that their country did nothing that requires compensation, or even apologies, and contend that many of the worst misdeeds their government has been accused of perpetrating never happened and that evidence that they did happen was fabricated by the Chinese and other Japan bashers."[5]

This is a case of those in power trying to rewrite history and to eradicate from the pages of history and from the memory of people the brutality the Japanese invaders perpetrated against the powerless people. A recent attempt at planting doubt in the minds of the younger Chinese generation about "the Rape of Nanking" during the war against China is found in the *New History Textbook* published in as recent as 2001. It touched lightly on the atrocity committed

4. See Chang, *Rape of Nanking*, 222.
5. Ibid.

by the Japanese soldiers and described it in a moderate tone (*ching miao tan shiee* in Chinese): "The Japanese army believed that when Nanking fell to it Chianag Kai-shek would surrender. When it succeeded in occupying Nanking in December [1937], it caused many casualties among the populace."[6] Nothing was said about how many noncombatants died, including children and how many women had been raped to death. The *New History Textbook* goes on to refer to the Far East International Military Tribunal held in Tokyo for two and half years that tried Japanese war criminals, saying that "the Tokyo Tribunal in question ascertained that the Japanese army killed many Chinese people at Nanking during the Japan-Chinese war (the Nanking Incident). Further, as to what had really happened, many questions still remain and different views expressed. The controversy continues even today."[7]

But will these attempts to cover up the atrocities succeed? No, they will not succeed. The stories of what happened will be told and remembered. These stories will be told again and again to become firmly etched in the collective human memory that no power on earth, even the power of those in power, can undo. When the Chinese city of Nanking fell to the victorious Japanese army on December 13, 1937,

> Japanese soldiers began an orgy of cruelty seldom if ever matched in world history. Tens of thousands of young men were rounded up and herded to the outer areas of the city, where they were mowed down by machine guns, used for bayonet practice, or soaked with gasoline and burned alive. For months the streets of the city were heaped with corpses and reeked with the stench of rotting human flesh. Years later experts at the International Military Tribunal of the Far East estimated that more than 260,000 noncombatants died at the hands of Japanese soldiers at Nanking in late 1937 and early 1938, though some experts have placed the figure at well over 350,000.[8]

THEOLOGY OF ELECTION

Does what happens in politics also happen in religion? Do religious authorities also do what political authorities do to rewrite history? Political ideology makes politicians, their supporters and theorists, distort the

6. Nishio, *New History Textbook*, 270.

7. Ibid., 295.

8. Chang, *Rape of Nanking*, 4.

truth of the matter. Do religious beliefs turned ideology lead religious leaders and teachers to do the same? Unfortunately, the answer is yes. If it happens in Christianity, it also happens in other religions. Theology rewrites stories to justify religious traditions, to defend particular beliefs, or to legitimize the religious power a certain group of believers has over others. This can become a source of religious conflict among people of the same faith and different faiths.

Within the Judeo-Christian tradition "the theology of election" has played a central role not only in the formation of faith but in the interpretation of history. It is the pivot around which the "sacred" history of Israel and Christianity revolves from ancient times to this day. It has served as the norm of excluding or including individuals, communities, tribes and nations in relation to the saving activity of God. Whether a history is sacred or not depends on how it measures against the theology of election. A story is sized up in the light of the theology of election. A history or a story is in this way "theologized." Theologization is an official process of elimination as well as of ratification. We have seen how it happened, for example, in ancient Greece and contemporary Japan. In religions, theologization of history and story is a norm rather than an exception. In the rest of this chapter we will see how this happens in both the Hebrew Bible and the New Testament. We will discuss in the next chapter how attempts are also made in both the Hebrew Bible and the New Testament to tell counter-stories and "de-theologize" what has been theologized.

"Jacob I loved but Esau I hated"

There are two personalities who have been made to play a crucial role in the theology of election. They are Jacob and Esau, the twin brothers born to Rebecca and Isaac. A prophet called Malachi in the fourth century BCE begins his discourse with what he declares to be "the oracle of the Lord to Israel." According to this oracle the Lord says:

> I have loved you, says the lord. But you say, "How have you loved us?" Is not Esau Jacob's brother? says the Lord. Yet I have loved Jacob, but I have hated Esau; I have made his hill country a desolation and his heritage a desert for jackals. (Mal 1:2–3)

Is this what God actually said? Or is it how Malachi interpreted the stories and histories related to Jacob and Esau and their descendants?

What is at the heart of this "oracle of the Lord" enunciated by the prophet Malachi is the theology of election. He reads the history of his people *backward* from the theology of election firmly embedded in the official faith and theology of his religious tradition. As he does this, what happens between the twin brothers Esau and Jacob is reshaped and retold to fit into the established patriarchal faith and theology. What theology often does is anachronistic, reading the past from the present and in the process distorting and misrepresenting the past. In spite of this, we can still recapture the story of the conflict between Jacob and Esau told in the Hebrew Bible so as to question the theology of election developed later.

What startles us is the fact that no less than Paul, the apostle to the Gentiles, embraces this theology of election when he wrestles with the question of the relation between Jews and Gentiles. This is what he says to the Christians at Rome in his letter:

> Even before they [Jacob and Esau] had been born or had done anything good or bad (so that God's purpose of election might continue, not by works but by his call) she [Rebecca] was told, "The elder shall serve the younger." As it is written,
> "I have loved Jacob,
>   but I have hated Esau." (Rom 9:11–13)

The Apostle Paul is here quoting Malachi's oracle of the Lord to underscore his theology of election. This is a very questionable argument, and coming from Paul, the apostle to the Gentiles, it is a bad argument.

The Apostle Paul does not stop here. He goes on to raise quite an ostentatious question and says:

> What then are we to say? Is there injustice on God's part? By no means! For God says to Moses:
>
> "I will have mercy on whom I have mercy,
> and I will have compassion on whom
> I have compassion."
>
> So it depends not on human will or exertion, but on God who shows mercy. (Rom 9:14–16)

What are we to make of his argument here?

Even though the Apostle Paul has parted company with his fellow Jewish Christians in Jerusalem, in this letter to the Christians in Rome he affirms the official theology of the history beginning with Abraham through Isaac and Jacob to the twelve patriarchs. In this scheme of the official theology of history, Esau is excluded and has no place in it. It is a *fait accompli.* This is a case of a theology rewriting history and reshaping what happened. Theology in this sense is a rewriting of history for a faith community for certain theological purposes.

The spread of the faith in Christ to the Roman world is a great missionary contribution the Apostle Paul has made. To carry out this mission he went through unspeakable suffering. As he tells us in his autobiographical account, "Five times I have received from the Jews the forty lashes minus one. Three times I was beaten with rods. I received a stoning. Three times I was shipwrecked; for a night and a day I was adrift at sea; on frequent journeys, in danger from rivers, danger from bandits, danger from my own people, danger from Gentiles, danger in the city, danger in the wilderness, danger at sea, danger from false brothers and sisters; in toil and hardship, through many a sleepless night, hungry and thirsty, often without food, cold and naked" (2 Cor 11:24–38).

Our hearts go out to the Apostle Paul. Is this not "mission impossible"? He may be exaggerating a little, but who among us can go through it all without despair and desperation? But even this Paul goes to the great length of interpreting the history of Esau's descendants and the "Gentiles," not only quoting with approval the words of an ancient prophet, but adding his own emphasis to it. Why did he not try to look at what happened to Esau and his descendants with the eyes of Gentile Christians?

A clue to this question can also be found in his other autobiographical accounts he made when he was rescued by the Roman guards from the angry mob in Jerusalem. "Brothers and fathers, listen to the defense that I now make before you," he begins his impassioned speech. "I am a Jew, born in Tarsus in Cilicia, but brought up in this city at the feet of Gamaliel, educated strictly according to our ancestral law, being jealous for God, just as all of you today . . ." Then he went on to tell them how he had been converted to Christ on his way to Damascus (Acts 22:1–21). His speech, instead of pacifying the mob, incited them all the more to call for his blood. My point here is that "the law," namely, "the theology" with which he was "educated strictly" at the feet of his great teacher Gamaliel continued to condition the ways in which he viewed Esau, his descendants, and the Gentiles "theologically." Even a man of astute theological insight like the Apostle Paul could not entirely shed the faith and theology that nurtured and shaped him.

But we cannot help asking: Did God really love Jacob and hate Esau? What kind of God loves one and hates the other? Is God's love a preferential kind of love? Is not this kind of God too much of a reflection of our likes and dislikes of us as human beings? God with such a preferential kind of love is not God, at least not Jesus' God. It takes deep insight into the nature of God for Jesus to be able to say to the religious authorities of his time: "Do not presume to say to yourselves, 'We have Abraham as our ancestor'; for I tell you, God is able from these stones to raise up children to Abraham" (Matt 3:9).

Yes, God loved Jacob and loves his descendants, but God also loves Esau and his descendants. If God loved Jacob and hated Esau, God would betray God's own nature. How could God be God if God betrayed God's own nature? How could God be God if God became not God? Furthermore, how could we human beings have the power to manipulate God and make God betray God's own nature? Would not that make us greater than God, not only like God but God? But even if we have that kind of power, which we do not have, Jesus is saying that "God is able from these stones to raise up children to Abraham"!

From these stones! Stones that you can see everywhere on the streets, along the roads, on the mountains and in the fields! Stones here in Palestine and outside Palestine! And stones are very common things, and humble things. Jesus once quoted Psalm 118 and likened himself to "the stone that the builders rejected." Stone is such a disposable thing. Its value depends totally on whether the builders would use it or not. If not used, it would be cast away without a second thought. But it is such a stone that has "become the cornerstone" (Matt 21:42). A dispensable stone becomes an indispensable stone! A disposable stone becomes an indisposable stone! This is what a cornerstone means in what Jesus says. If Jacob is such a cornerstone, is not Esau also such a cornerstone? If the descendants of Jacob are such cornerstones, are not the descendants of Esau also such cornerstones?

If this fundamental insight into the nature of God's love is not grasped by theologians in ancient Israel, neither is it understood by most Christian theologians. They have done exactly what theologians in ancient Israel did, rewriting the stories of nations and peoples outside the Christian church and developing the theology of "salvation history" based almost entirely on what the Apostle Paul said about God being partial to Jacob and prejudiced towards Esau. That is why there are very few stories of nations and peoples in theological writings. And when nations and peoples appear in these writings, they are either marginalized or compromised in the interest of Christianity being the only way to God's saving love. What one mostly has in these Christian theological writings is theological and doctrinal inferences from the premises of the doctrine of God's election.

The Potter and the Clay

That God has elected some people for salvation and others for condemnation has been the main emphasis of the teaching of the Christian church. Most theology and practice of mission has been built on this doctrinal premise. Under such a doctrinal premise stories of people outside Christianity seeking fulfillment of life and the bliss of salvation are almost entirely rejected as justification by works over against justification by faith.

Augustine uses the biblical metaphor of the potter and the clay to explain how God elects some and rejects others. According to him:

> There was one lump of perdition (*massa perditionis*) out of Adam to which only punishment was due; from this same lump, vessels were made which are destined for honor, for the potter has authority over the same lump of clay (Romans 9:21). What lump? The lump that had already perished, and whose just damnation was already assured. So, be thankful that you have escaped! You have escaped the death certainly due to you, and found life, which was not due to you. The potter has authority over the clay from the same lump to make one vessel for honor and another for contempt. But, you say, why has He made me for honor and another for contempt? What shall I answer? Will you listen to Augustine, if you will not listen to the Apostle [Paul] when he says: "O man, who art you who argues with God?" (Romans 11:33). Two little children are born. If you ask what is due to them, the answer is that they both belong to the lump of perdition. But why does its mother carry the one to grace, while the other is suffocated by its mother in her sleep? Will you tell me what was deserved by the one who was carried to grace, and what was deserved by the one whom its sleeping mother suffocated? Both have deserved nothing good; but the potter has authority over the clay, of the same lump to make one vessel for honor, and the other for contempt.[9]

9. See "Augustine on the Divine Election," in McGrath, *Christian Theology Reader*, 217.

This is a good example of theology rewriting story to suit a theological assertion.

The metaphor of the potter and the clay has biblical references. It is used by the prophets Jeremiah, Second Isaiah and Malachi in the Hebrew Bible and the Apostle Paul in the New Testament. Both Isaiah and Jeremiah use the metaphor to make the point of how God deals with people with compassion and not in punishment. Let us first look at the reference to God as the potter made by Jeremiah. These are the words from the Lord that inspired him to grasp what we will now call "theology of history":

> The Word that came to Jeremiah from the Lord: "Come, go down to the potter's house, and there I will let you hear my words." So I went down to the potter's house, and there he was working at his wheel. The vessel he was making of clay was spoiled in the potter's hand, and he reworked it into another vessel, as seemed good to him. (Jer 18:1–4)

This is a common scene at a pottery. The potter plays an active role while the clay a passive role. Who is in control, the potter or the clay? Of course the potter! The potter molds, shapes and fashions the clay into something he desires and envisions. If the clay does not turn out to be something he has wanted, it is not the clay's fault. It is entirely the potter's fault. He has no choice but to do it all over again until he achieves his purpose. The clay is entirely compliant, having no say in what the potter is doing to it.

What concerns Jeremiah most, as it turns out, is not the potter working the clay. What he sees at the pottery inspires him to make a leap of faith, likening God to the potter and comparing nations to the clay. As he does this, the active and passive roles of the potter and the clay undergo subtle changes, although Jeremiah himself may not be aware of the change. Let us find out how his "theology of the potter and the clay" makes a sudden departure from what he sees at the pottery. As he tells us,

> Then the word of the Lord came to me: "Can I not do with you, O house of Israel, just as the potter has done? Just as the clay in the potter's hand, so are you in my hand, O house of Israel. At one moment I may declare concerning a nation or a kingdom, that I will pluck up and break down and destroy it, but if that nation . . . turns from its evil, I will change my mind about the disaster

that I intended to bring on it. And at another moment I may
declare concerning a nation or a kingdom that I will build and
plant it, but if it does evil in my sight . . . I will change my mind
about the good that I intended to do to it. (Jer 18:5–10)

In this "theology of the potter and the clay" the potter is no longer in
total control of the clay, nor the clay merely playing a passive role. The
potter and the clay become interactive. The clay, standing for Israel and
other nations, can be active enough to change the ways in which God
deals with them.

The Prophet Jonah and the City of Nineveh

In this theological inference derived from what he has seen at the pottery,
Jeremiah makes a vital change in his theology of election. Whether he is
conscious of it or not, in his continuing discourse God as potter is no
longer capable of molding, shaping and fashioning a nation as God desires and chooses. God the potter can no longer do whatever God wants
with a nation as the potter does with the clay. God may still be compared
to the potter, but a nation is not as passive as the clay, as compliant as the
clay. The ball is in the court of a particular nation, as it were. What God
may do with it depends on whether it turns from evil or not.

This reminds us of the story of Jonah at the Assyrian city of Nineveh.
When its people, from the king to the citizens, alarmed by Jonah's
doomsday warning, "believed God, proclaimed a fast, put on sackcloth"
(Jonah 3:5–6), expressing their remorse and repentance, "God changed
God's mind about the calamity that God had said God would bring upon
them" (3:10). The people of Nineveh repented and God did change God's
mind as God had said God would.

For Jonah this is too much. His theology of election is not only
severely strained but falls apart. To the distraught and angry Jonah, God
says: "Should I not be concerned about Nineveh, that great city, in which
there are more than 120,000 persons who do not know their right hand
from their left, and also many animals?" (4:11) The author of the book
of Jonah, ending his story this way, does not sound conclusive. But he
seems to be saying that the theology of election developed in the official
theology of Israel and Judah does not have the chance to stand the test
of history and the vicissitudes of the nations, including Israel and Judah.
Did not Israel and Judah perish at the hands of the foreign nations?

The Prophet Exiled in Babylon

We cannot help but realize that the parable of the potter and the clay has undergone a fundamental change that questions the theology of election. This seems also the case with the prophet exiled in Babylon with his fellow Jews. We do not know his name, but he has left us with some most insightful observations of what he perceives to be God at work among the nations. At one point he also uses the imagery of the potter and clay when he says:

> Yet, O Lord, you are our Father;
> we are the clay, and you are our potter,
> we are still the work of your hand. (Isa 64:8)

What prompts him to evoke the potter and clay imagery to remind the reader of the relationship between God and Judah? Is it not something similar to what Jeremiah has to reckon with when confronted with the adverse history of his nation?

The prophet in exile is faced with the collapse of the metaphor of God as the potter and the people of Judah as the clay. The destruction of Jerusalem with its holy temple is a fact. That he and many of his compatriots are taken to Babylon as exiles and spend their time in captivity is also a fact. He has to recognize that the relation between God and God's people has shifted. The nations and peoples outside Israel and Judah have come to play an increasingly significant role in God's activity among the nations.

Has not the prophet, known as Second Isaiah, perceived this irrevocable change? Observing the historical realities that followed the downfall of his own nation, he has enunciated these memorable words:

> The Lord says of Cyrus, "He is my shepherd,
> and he shall carry out all my purpose." (Isa 44:28)

This is a most daring thing to say when Cyrus, king of Persia, is identified as God's shepherd to carry out God's purpose.

But the prophet in question does not stop there. He goes on to say something that must have astounded his fellow exiles, something that has totally upset the official theology of election:

> Thus says the Lord to his anointed, to Cyrus,
> whose right hand I have grasped,
> to subdue nations before him

and to strip kings of their robes,
to open doors before him—
and the gates shall not be closed . . . (45:1)

This is an astonishing thing to say, calling Cyrus, king of Persia, "God's anointed."

It should be noted that Cyrus, a pagan king, is called "God's anointed" to carry out the purpose of God to bring the Jewish exiles back to Jerusalem. Yes, Cyrus did just that, and a great many exiles did return to Jerusalem. But the history of the Jewish people as a nation continued to decline until it was destroyed by the Roman armies in 70 CE. That prophet in exile had to remind God, almost in desperation, that they as the clay are still the work of God the potter (Isa 64:8b), but God is no longer able to prevent them from meeting their historical fate of destruction.

It is extremely significant that the enunciation of Cyrus as God's anointed is preceded by the confession of God as creator. In the prophet's own words, this is what the Lord says:

I am the Lord who made all things,
who alone stretched out the heavens,
who by myself stretched out the earth . . . (Isa 44:24)

God the creator looms large in the prophet's theology of history. When this shift has taken place from the theology of redemption to the theology of creation, it is inevitable that the official theology of election comes under scrutiny. As to Christianity, its theology of salvation, with Christianity having a privileged place in God's saving activity, needs to yield to a theology oriented toward all nations.

What we have seen and discussed are some examples, both within the Christian Bible and outside it, of how theology, and for that matter, ideology, has a strong tendency to domesticate stories, remold them and rewrite them, as the potter shapes and reshapes the clay, to serve its beliefs, teachings and claims. How do we then restore integrity to stories and let them speak with their own voices? In other words, how can stories be freed from theological control and ideological domination? Our purpose is to explore this question in this book. In the next chapter we will see how Jesus goes about rectifying official theologies with the stories in which he becomes involved personally.

4

Stories Rectify Theology

IT HAS TO BE emphasized that the separation of theology and story in traditional theology is unwarranted and misguided. Does not the Christian Bible consist mostly of stories? It is the same with scriptures of other religions. Do not worshippers, while they do not remember doctrinal claims of the preachers, remember the stories they tell, if they tell pointed and moving stories in their sermons? Why is it? Is it because a story is funny? Is it because it is amusing? Is it because it is thought-provoking? Is it because they empathize with it? Is it because it touches the sore spot in their conscience? Is it because it makes them think deep thought about who they are and what they are? Is it because it challenges them to give thought to their destiny?

It must be that all these, and even more, reasons combine to make a story play a critical role in our life. In essence, story has to do with life, a real life, a life you and I live in this world. Your life and mine consist of stories from the moment we were born to the moment we die. Life is made up of endless stories, stories of hope and despair, of joy and sorrow, of victory and defeat, of success and failure, and of life and death. Stories emerge from life, accompany life, even change life. Do stories change life? Yes, they do. Do we not sometimes hear stories that change people's lives? And perhaps your life has been changed because of some stories that have challenged you and moved you.

Is it, therefore, not evident that theology divorced from stories is not theology, if theology is closely bound with life? But is there a theology not bound with life, whether it is God's life or people's lives? Theologians have this strong urge to shape life, be it God's life or human life, dictate it, and dominate it. That is why they often rewrite stories that do not suit their purposes, as we have seen in the previous chapter. But theologians who rewrite a story betray the story, and as they do this, they betray their vocation to give account of what happens in God's creation and in human community.

In this chapter we will discuss how stories of Jesus rectify the theologies held sacrosanct by his own religious traditions and authorities.

JESUS AN UNCOMMON RABBI

Jesus is a very uncommon rabbi (teacher), although some do address him as rabbi. Two disciples of John the Baptizer get curious about him and start to follow him. They address him as rabbi (teacher), then ask him where he is staying (John 1:35–39).

My impression is that Jesus never likes people calling him rabbi. Once he admonishes his followers, saying: "You are not to be called rabbis." Why? This is the reason he gives: "for you have one teacher, and you are all students" (Matt 23:8–9). Who is this one teacher to whom we, regardless of who we are, are students? It is God! God is our Rabbi, our supreme Teacher. No one should pretend to know what God knows, not to mention, more than what God knows. Already here Jesus is using a particular situation to dispute the age-old assumption that learned religious leaders are more qualified than ordinary men and women to know what God has in store for them.

Rabbi or not, Jesus speaks, teaches and practices about the rule of God with an authority never seen before. One Sabbath in Capernaum, after he has spoken at the synagogue, people "are astounded at his teaching, for he has taught them as one having authority, and not as the scribes" (Mark 1:22). People have sensed something uncommon in this unconventional rabbi and cannot help comparing him with the stereotyped discourses on the law given by their rabbis. What makes his teaching astounding? It is his way of relating God's stories to their own life stories and their life stories to God's stories. For the first time in their life of faith, they realize that stories, and not doctrines, build bridges between them and God. It is through stories, theirs or those of others, that God gets related to them and they to God. And there is story after story in the Gospels showing how Jesus enables people to gain new glimpses of God in their life stories.

A NEW TEACHING!

There is a story of Jesus healing a deranged man in the synagogue, a story that has, as we have seen, stirred people and inspired them to recognize in Jesus a very unconventional rabbi (Mark 1:23–28). As the story goes,

> there was in their synagogue a man with an unclean spirit, and he cried out, "What have you to do with us, Jesus of Nazareth? Have you come to destroy us? I know who you are, the Holy One of God." But Jesus rebuked him, saying, "Be silent, and come out of him!" And the unclean spirit, convulsing him and crying with a loud voice, came out of him. They were all amazed, and they kept on asking one another, "What is this? A new teaching with authority!"

The whole synagogueA drama must have been thrown first into confusion and then jubilation!

What makes people in the synagogue exclaim in surprise what they have witnessed as a new teaching with authority? In this story, at least in the way Mark tells it, Jesus has not taught in so many words why the man had an unclean spirit. He has not gone into great length to explain what that unclean spirit might be. He immediately goes into action and restores sanity to the man. This is not what people expect from their rabbis. Their rabbis would tell them that this man with an unclean spirit is clear evidence of God's punishment of the sins he has committed. He has therefore to repent first before anything can be done for him. But if the man is punished by God, how can anyone, including their religious leaders, heal him? It is up to God to heal him or not, since it is God who has imposed punishment on him.

But the story of Jesus healing this man with an unclean spirit turns upside down this traditional belief in the undisputable law of causality between this man's derangement and God's punishment. That is not what they are accustomed to hear from their rabbis in the synagogue. That is not what their religious leaders have led them to believe. This healing story does not say a word about the belief and teaching that everyone has taken for granted, but it refutes them with great power. Actions speak louder than words, as the saying goes. Jesus' actions always speak louder than the words of the religious authorities.

What is a story if not a drama or a play? It is not just words; it is words dramatized, played, and acted out on the stage, be it the stage of a theater or the stage of life. On that particular Sabbath in the synagogue, the people are confronted with a story, a drama, a play, acted out between Jesus and the man with an unclean spirit. They are at a loss for words what to say. All they can do is to exclaim spontaneously: "A new teaching with authority!" Mark deserves to be called a skillful and ingenious storyteller. He has the story of what happened in the synagogue unfold in rapid succession, and it rectifies the official theology regarding illness as God's punishment of human sin.

THE STORY OF THE MAN BORN BLIND

Another powerful example of how a story can rectify theology is to be found in the story of Jesus restoring sight to the man born blind (John 9:1–34). We already referred to it in the previous chapter, but here we take up this story once again in greater detail to show how Jesus rectifies the conventional faith and the official theology of his own religion.

What we have here is not just another healing story. Each healing story of Jesus has a singular point special to it. And there is something special in this story of Jesus healing the man born blind. This point will become evident presently as we compare this story with the story of Jesus raising Lazarus.

There is no question about the fact that John is a superb storyteller as well as a first-rate theologian. He is not only capable of profound theological reflection as he has demonstrated in the prologue (John 1:1–18). He also knows how to tell stories to question age-old theological stereotypes. The story of Jesus restoring sight to the man born blind is one of these stories. In this respect there is no match for this story in the rest of the Gospel.

One may not quite agree, though, citing instead the story of Jesus raising Lazarus from death (John 11:1–44). But as you read these two stories, you cannot but notice some basic differences. The story of Jesus raising Lazarus from death is slightly longer than the story of him restoring sight to the man born blind, but less dramatic. The story does not conceal the author's theology of resurrection; that theology is obvious from the start. The story begins with Jesus being told about Lazarus' illness (11:3), but the author does not wait for his theology of resurrection to develop by itself. He immediately has Jesus say: "This illness does not lead to death; rather it is for God's glory, so that the Son of God may be glorified through it" (11:4). From there the story sails towards the end without a hitch, punctuated by theological statements along the way. When Martha, one of Lazarus' sisters, meets Jesus in great distress, Jesus declares: "I am the resurrection and the life. Those who believe in me, even though they die, will live" (11:25–26). From this point on the story is told to support the theology of resurrection. Jesus calling Lazarus out of the tomb is in fact an anti-climax, preceded by his prayer to God: "Father, I thank you for having heard me. I knew that you always hear me, but I have said this for the sake of the crowd standing here, so that they may believe that you sent me" (11:41–43). The emphasis of the story is evident: not to demonstrate how Jesus raises Lazarus from death but to show why people should believe in Jesus, "the word of God," in whom "was life" (1:4). Obviously, this is an example of how a story serves the theological purpose of an author.

It is quite different with the story of Jesus restoring sight to the man born blind. There are twists and turns in the story and you are not quite sure how the story is going to turn out at the end. There are several theological elements in the story, but they are embedded in it and not quite obvious. You are left in suspense until the very end before it dawns on you what the author is driving at theologically. Suspense! Is a story still a story without suspense? Suspense is the vital force of a good story. Without it a story is an endless tale unable to arouse the interest and inspire the imagination of its reader.

Another important difference between the story of Jesus raising Lazarus from death and the story of Jesus restoring sight to the man born blind is this: in the first story Jesus, and not Lazarus, is the main actor, while in the second story it is not Jesus but the man born blind. Lazarus does not say a word from beginning to end; it is Jesus speaking most of the time, enunciating theological points one after another. In the other story the main speaker is the man born blind. He dominates the controversy between him and the religious authorities. Even after he has defended himself before the religious authorities, he does not conceal the fact that he does not know the man who has restored his sight. When he returns to Jesus, he is still asking Jesus who has restored sight to him. In the Lazarus story, Lazarus has only a shadowy existence. He is dead! In the man-born-blind story, it is not so. The man is very much alive, making sure he is heard by all parties aroused by his extraordinary experience. In contrast to the Lazarus story, this story gives birth to theological claims as it moves from one scene to another, rectifying along the way the theology that has dominated the religious authorities and believers for centuries.

It happens as follows. The stage is set when "Jesus saw a man blind from birth" on the road he is traveling with his disciples (John 9:1). The first to speak is not Jesus but the disciples. They ask him: "Rabbi, who sinned, this man or his parents, that he was born blind?" (9:2) The theological premise is thus set, the premise of faith the disciples have inherited from their religious traditions, the premise reiterated by the religious authorities from one generation to the next.

It has to be noted that although the disciples cast their belief in the form of a question, what they are seeking is a confirmation from Jesus of what their teachers and all other people have always believed. In a basic belief such as this, they are not expecting a different reply from Jesus, their rabbi. It must have, therefore, taken the disciples by surprise when Jesus addresses their question and says: "Neither this man nor his parents sinned; he was born blind so that God's work might be revealed in him" (9:3).

Two positions are set in striking contrast: the disciples' and Jesus'. For the disciples the blindness of the man is caused if not by his own sin, then by his parents' sin, but most likely by the sins of both. He has sinned and has to bear the consequences of having been born blind, but at the same time his sin is part of the sin he has inherited from his parents or from his forebears. The responsibility of the sin one has committed always contradicts the belief in the inherited sin. If the sin is inherited, in theory one is not responsible for it, although one has to suffer the consequences of it. There is no way to get away from the contradiction. Despite the contradiction this is how believers are taught to believe for generations.

Jesus has nothing to do with this belief. He refutes it head-on when he declares categorically: "Neither this man nor his parents sinned; he was born blind so that God's works might be revealed in him." Then he proceeds to spread the mud mixed with his saliva over the man's eyes and ask the man to wash in the pool of Siloam. As the man has done what he is told, his eyesight is restored to him (9:6–7).

What has occurred is nothing short of astonishing, but this is just a part of the prelude with which the story begins, the premise of the disciples' question and Jesus' reply. The real drama is to begin after this rather conventional start. From here on the story develops into several scenes, each scene filled with suspense. Suspense, as we have said before, is one of the most important factors for a good story.

Scene One: "I am the man!"

In this first scene the neighbors are simply astonished and then become curious. They have known the man for a long time as a blind beggar, but he can now see. This is incredible! The following conversation takes place among them about the man who has become the subject of their intense interest:

> "Is this not the man who used to sit and beg?"
> "It is he."
> "No, but it is someone like him."

There must be great confusion, but the man who has his eyesight restored to him says resolutely:

> "I am the man."

His neighbors are still not convinced. They still want to know how he has his eyesight restored. To this the man responds:

> "The man called Jesus made mud, spread it on my eyes, and said
> to me, 'Go to Siloam and wash.' Then I went and washed and
> received my sight."

The curiosity of their neighbors now turns to the person who has made the man see again. They ask him: "Where is he?" To this question he gives an honest answer:

> "I do not know."

He does not know. He truly does not know. He seems as bewildered as his neighbors.

Scene Two: "He is a prophet"

Their curiosity not allayed, they do the next best thing, taking the man to the religious authorities, to have their religious leaders deal with their question. With the man who professed to have his eyesight restored to him and the agitated crowd in front of them, the religious leaders proceed to find out what happened. When the man repeated once again how he had received his sight, they are incredulous at first and then become irritated. They tell the man:

"'This man is not from God, for he does not observe the Sabbath
... How can a man who is a sinner perform such sign. What do
you say about him?" (9:16–17)

The theology of the sabbath! This is the theology the religious leaders
have inherited from the past. It is the core of their religious tradition. It
is the heart of the religious piety they demand from the believers. This
theology of the sabbath is greater and more important than their theology of God. Even God has to observe the law of the sabbath! A person has
broken the law of the sabbath; the healer is therefore a sinner. It stands
to reason that a sinner cannot perform a sign of restoring the eyesight of
a man born blind. It is simply impossible; it is even blasphemous.

Did Jesus happen to heal the blind man on the sabbath? Or did he
do it on purpose? Whether by coincidence or on purpose Jesus must be
aware that he is infringing upon the time-honored law of the sabbath.
As to the man questioned by the religious authorities, all their questions
are not important. Even the question of who has healed his blindness is
not important. As a matter of fact, he cannot identify the man who has
healed him. He can only answer the questions posed by the religious
leaders, saying:

"He is a prophet." (9:17)

In his simple religious mind, a prophet is someone who can work miracles. That he can now see is nothing short of a miracle. He therefore
concludes that the man who restored sight to him is a prophet.

Scene Three: "He is of age; ask him"

The religious leaders are not about to let the matter rest at that. Too
much is at stake in their authority as religious leaders, in their religious
tradition, and in their theology of the sabbath. Finding the man not co
operating with them, they turn to his parents to elicit the answer they
are looking for. When the parents arrive for questioning, the following
exchange takes place between them and the man's parents (9:19–21):

Religious leaders: "Is this your son, who you say was born blind?
How then does he now see?"
The parents: "We know this is our son, and that he was born
blind, but we do not know how it is that now he sees, nor do we
know who opened his eyes. Ask him; he is of age. He will speak
for himself."

The parents know the religious leaders have already made up their minds that "anyone who confessed Jesus to be the Messiah would be put out of the synagogue" (9:22). This is a very serious matter not only for the man's parents but for all believers. Put out of the synagogue, they become social and religious pariahs, abandoned by their society and religious community. They would become nobody, shunned by their fellow believers. Does not this sound strangely similar to the theology of the Christian church that "outside the church there is no salvation"?

The parents are frightened. Who would not be in the same situation? This is the theology that justifies violent use of power against powerless people like the man's parents. Such theology has to be rectified. But how? By developing an alternative doctrine, teaching or belief? No, this is not the approach taken by John, the storyteller. He takes time to let the story unfold itself to question the theology that justifies the use of power to intimidate people without power into submission.

First, John has the parents acknowledge the fact that the man who regained his sight is indeed their son. How can they deny this plain fact without disowning their son? But they know their limits in front of the religious authorities. There is a line they cannot cross without antagonizing the people who hold power over them. They have to admit that they know neither how their son is now able to see nor who opened his eyes. This may be a weak defense to save their own skins; it contains a subtle defiance when they tell the religious leaders: "Ask him; he is of age. He will speak for himself." Can you hear an undertone in these words? With these words the parents are letting the onus of proof fall upon the religious authorities. These words leave no alternative but for them to turn to the man once again.

Scene Four: "One thing I do know . . ."

The drama reaches its climax when the man is called back to the religious authorities for further questioning. The verbal exchange between them is lively and breathtaking. As it progresses, it puts the religious leaders more and more on the defensive and the man more and more on the offensive. This is all the more astonishing because the position is reversed: armed with the truth, the powerless man gains power over the powerful religious authorities. You may call the power the man gains a moral power. In contrast the power held by the religious leaders becomes an immoral power. It is this moral power of a single person triumphing over the immoral power of a religious institution that the storyteller seems to celebrate in the ensuing exchanges (9:24–34):

> Religious leaders: "Give glory to God! We know that this man is a sinner."
>
> The man: "I do not know whether he is a sinner. One thing I do know, that though I was blind, now I see."
>
> Religious leaders: "What did he do to you? How did he open your eyes?"
>
> The man: "Why do you want to hear it again? Do you also want to become his disciples?"
>
> Religious leaders: (reviling him, saying) "You are his disciple, but we are disciples of Moses, but as for this man, we do not know where he comes from."
>
> The man: "Here is an astonishing thing! You do not know where he comes from, and yet he opened my eyes. We know that God does not listen to sinners, but he does listen to the one who worships him and obeys his will. Never since the world began has it been heard that anyone opened the eyes of a person born blind. If this man were not from God, he could do nothing."
>
> Religious leaders:"You were born entirely in sin, and are you trying to teach us?" (And they drove him out.)

This longest exchange is the highlight of the entire story. It is filled with tension, almost making one "break out into cold perspiration" (*nhie yi ba han* in Chinese), as one wonders what the outcome is going to be for the man facing the religious authorities. The religious leaders' assertions are stereotyped, while the man's response is quick and sharp. John succeeds in letting a layperson lay out basic beliefs and convictions so vividly and brilliantly that it makes the theology of the religious leaders pale and weak.

Here we have the theology of people conceived in this section of the story that rectifies the official theology of the religious authorities. The story makes it clear that a real fact speaks more eloquently than an abstract truth, that experience precedes ideas or concepts, the moral power of even a lone individual, and not the immoral power of those in power and authority, determines what truth is. Evidently the religious leaders have lost in this heated exchange. All they can do is to resort to the institutional power they have "to drive the man out," another demonstration of the violent use of the power they claim to have inherited from Moses, their great ancestor.

Scene Five: Lord, I believe!

The man who has his sight restored is excommunicated by the religious authorities, but has he been thus reduced to a spiritual nobody? On the contrary! He is alienated from the religious establishment only to find a new spiritual home in the person who opened his eyes. As the story reaches this happy end, it rectifies the official theology of the synagogue fortified with beliefs, creeds and traditions—with a theology of the community of believers around Jesus and around his ministry of the rule of God. The story thus concludes with the deeply soul-searching talk between Jesus and the man who received his sight from Jesus (9:35–38):

> Jesus: "Do you believe in the Son of Man?"
>
> The man: "And who is he, sir? Tell me, so that I may believe in him."
>
> Jesus: "You have seen him, and the one speaking with you is he."
>
> The man: "Lord, I believe."

The story reaches its end as the man confesses his faith in Jesus, saying: "Lord, I believe." At this point John the storyteller gives way to John the theologian when he has Jesus say: "I came into this world for judgment so that those who do not see may see, and those who do see may become blind" (9:30–41).

The genius of this story is not the theological verdict made by John the storyteller. The story waits almost to the end for the man to confess faith in Jesus. His confession of faith in Jesus is not the presupposition of the story but the outcome of it, not the premise on which the story is told but the conclusion developed from the story. The story, after long suspenseful twists and turns, finally succeeds in replacing the official theology of who the messiah is with a theology that has grown out of the direct person-to-person relationship between Jesus and the man to whom Jesus has restored sight.

THOSE WHO LOVE MUCH ARE FORGIVEN MUCH

People are in need of forgiveness from one another. This is a fact of life that no one can deny. Even if you do not commit a crime that sends you to prison, you have often done something against others that makes you feel guilty and remorseful. You do not have peace of mind until you have received forgiveness from the person you have wronged or offended.

If forgiveness is essential to the wellness of human relationships, it is even more so in our relationship with God. Forgiveness is thus the heart of Christianity and almost all religions. Did not the people of ancient Israel offer sin offerings to seek forgiveness from their God? Do not Christians confess their sins to God during the worship service? Do not Buddhists burn incense at the temple to appease their gods?

What motivates believers to be engaged in such religious acts? First of all, it is the ignorance of the forces at work in nature, in life and beyond nature and life. These forces are invisible but hard to grasp. They are incomprehensible and yet real when they affect movements of nature and courses of life. Polytheism, the worship of many gods, is, in a sense, to make sure that no supernatural force, known or unknown, especially an unknown one, is left out in the homage and tribute the devotees pay to it.

With ignorance comes fear. We fear the enemies hiding in the dark prepared to strike us. We fear the malicious people plotting to harm us behind our back. We fear what is going to happen to us because we do not know what is waiting for us. Above all, we fear gods we can neither see nor touch but who control our life and our fate. And why does a disaster strike us and our community without warning, plunging our lives and community into great tragedies? This makes us fear all the more the gods who bring us disaster and misfortune. It is not without reason that fear is considered to be one of the intrinsic causes that make people resort to religious activities.

What people are most afraid of is punishment for what they have done. We fear the punishment of our teachers for not doing homework. We fear punishment of our parents when we disobey their demands. We fear punishment (or retaliation) when we have offended someone. And we are afraid of gods' punishment for the offense we have committed against gods, whether knowingly or unknowingly. Gods have, therefore, to be placated with repentance, penance, offering and worship.

In this way, forgiveness is central to Christianity as it is also central to most other religions. But forgiveness is not given completely free. It can be given only after believers have performed various kinds of religious rituals, some very elaborate, and certain ceremonies, some very intricate. It becomes obvious that these elaborate rituals and intricate ceremonies require "experts" to devise them and conduct them. Is this how powerful hierarchy of priesthood and clergy came not only to dominate the religious community but often the social and political life of a nation?

If people of all ages and all places have to reckon with the religious institution, with its theology and practice of forgiveness, Jesus too is confronted with it in the hierarchy of his own religion. Early on in his ministry he realizes that one cannot change the theology of the established religion by developing another set of theological propositions and doctrinal assertions. Instead, he finds in stories a powerful instrument to rectify the theology of the establishment, in this particular case, the theology of God's forgiveness. It is not ignorance, fear, punishment, that constitutes the heart of forgiveness. It is love! How does Jesus relate this story of divine forgiveness to people around him? This is what we are going to see in this story of "the woman with the ointment" in the Gospels.

THE WOMAN WITH A JAR OF COSTLY OINTMENT

This story must have left such a deep impression on quite a few people that Matthew, Mark, Luke, and John have all included it in their Gospels, although details of the story vary in the Gospels (Matt 26:6–13; Mark 14:3–9; Luke 7:36–50; John 12:1–8). For Matthew and Mark the incident takes place in the house of Simon the leper in Bethany to which Jesus has been invited for supper. In John's version the supper takes place in the house of Lazarus and his sisters, Martha and Mary. While they are having supper, a woman (Mary, according to John; is it Mary, the sister of Martha and Lazarus?) appears with an alabaster jar of very costly ointment (Matt 26:7; Mark 14:3–9; John 12:3).

From the development of the story, Matthew, Mark and John, the three authors of the Gospels, all make the point of how expensive the ointment is. This leads to the disciples' bitter complaint, even strong protest, that the woman has wasted it all and that the money she has spent on the oil could have been given to the poor. Their complaint and protest prompts Jesus to commend what she has done as a beautiful thing (Mark 14:6; Matt 26:10) in anticipation of his death (Matt 26:12; John 12:7). At the same time he reminds them that they can help the poor whenever they want to but they are soon to lose him (Matt 26:11; Mark 14:7; John 12:8). Mark and Matthew end the story with Jesus' celebrated statement: "Truly I tell you, wherever the good news is proclaimed in the whole world, what she has done will be told in remembrance of her" (Mark 14:9; Matt 26:13).

Supper at the Pharisee's Home

The story told by Luke in his Gospel is quite different both in detail and in intention. First, the supper takes place in the house of one of the Pharisees by the name of Simon. This at once lays the groundwork for the development of the story in a very different direction. As the story develops, you realize it is not the question of poverty that is at issue, but the question of forgiveness. By having the supper take place in a Pharisee's house and with the ensuing exchange between Jesus and Simon the Pharisee, Luke tells a story to rectify the theology of forgiveness long held by the religious hierarchy and the religious community.

The story goes on to describe graphically what the woman has done after she enters the house with a jar of costly ointment. "She stood behind Jesus at his feet, weeping," so says the story, "and began to bathe his feet with her tears and to dry them with her hair. Then she continued kissing his feet and anointing them with the ointment" (Luke 7:38). Apparently, these expressions of affection and devotion are too much for Simon the Pharisee. Luke captures this uneasiness on the part of Simon the Pharisee by having the latter say to himself: "If this man [Jesus] were a prophet, he would have known who and what kind of woman this is who is touching him—that she is a sinner" (7:39). Is this a mere murmur, mere discomfort, mere uneasiness? The storyteller has Simon the Pharisee say these words not merely to have him express displeasure and disapproval of what the woman is doing to Jesus. Implied in these words is the official theology of forgiveness. It asserts that this woman, since everyone in town knows that she is a sinner, does not deserve God's forgiveness. Moreover, not knowing who she is, this man called Jesus discredits himself as a prophet.

Sensing what his host is saying to himself, Jesus is not about to let him get away with his theology. And at this point the story takes a dramatic turn as Jesus initiates the conversation with his host (7:40–47):

Jesus: "I have something to say to you."

The Pharisee: "Teacher, speak."

Jesus: "A certain creditor had two debtors; one owed five hundred denarii [a denarius was about a day's wage] and the other fifty. When they could not pay, he canceled the debts for both of them. Now which of them will love him more?"

> The Pharisee: "I suppose the one for whom he canceled the greater debt."
>
> Jesus: "You have judged rightly." (Then turning toward the woman, he said to Simon): "Do you see this woman? I entered your house; you gave me no water for my feet, but she has bathed my feet with her tears and dried them with her hair. You gave me no kiss, but from the time I came in she has not stopped kissing my feet. You did not anoint my head with oil, but she has anointed my feet with ointment."

I cannot help wondering how Simon the Pharisee reacted to what Jesus had said to him. Every word Jesus has said to him is true and must have gone to his heart. Is he embarrassed? Is he offended? Does he retort in objection? We do not know, for Luke the storyteller has not told us. But what else could he have said about the story of the two debtors other than what he has said? He must have quickly realized that it has a powerful pertinence to the situation he has found himself in. How could he then object to what the woman had done to Jesus? The woman in the midst of his guests is more grateful to God than Simon the Pharisee. She is much more deeply aware of her need for God's forgiveness than he is.

What Luke the storyteller has told us is already more than a story; it is a story theology. It is a story that rectifies the official theology of God's forgiveness, and it is a story that points to the relationship between God and human beings based on love and forgiveness. Any theology of forgiveness derived from fear and punishment is a wrong theology. The theology that pays attention to the stories of how people experience God's forgiveness is the right theology. In this sense this story told by Luke anticipates the story of Jesus' cross, on which love and forgiveness, both human and divine, work together to become the most painful yet most beautiful story every told, as the Gospels of Matthew and Mark have rightly concluded towards the end of the story of the woman with an alabaster jar of costly oil.

"She has shown great love!"

Forgiveness and love; love and forgiveness! What the woman who anoints Jesus has done is to show how much she loves because she has been forgiven much. And as she has been forgiven much, she is able to love much. Those who have not experienced forgiveness cannot love, and those who cannot love have not experienced forgiveness. If this is so between one human being and another, it must be even more so between God and us human beings.

This moving story is another example of how Jesus, in his ministry of God's rule, tells a story in the daily life of people to rectify the age-old beliefs and theological traditions of his own religion. Furthermore, he lets stories of people disclose how God responds to the pain and joy, suffering and hope of men and women who struggle to find God's saving love despite the religion that judges and condemns them. He also tells stories to help them know that the loving God is ultimately the meaning of their life in this all too ephemeral world. What Jesus says to Simon the Pharisee at the end of the story brings in to focus the central concern of faith and theology. "Therefore," he says to his host, "her sins, which were many, have been forgiven; hence she has shown great love. But the one to whom little is forgiven, loves little" (7:47).

Love is the power in this story. It has to be the power of stories that moves people and changes them. The theology that emerges out of stories of love is a powerful theology. It is this powerful theology that Jesus has developed from stories—stories of women, men, and children with whom he associates himself, his own stories, and stories of how God is involved with human life and community. Jesus' theology is story theology, and a powerful story theology at that. In the next chapter we will explore this power that makes theology powerful.

5

The Theological Power of Stories

THE STORY THAT RECTIFIES the faith and theology sanctioned by the religious authorities must be equipped with power. It is not just any kind of power, but a power that carries out God's purpose for the world and serves the well-being of people. It is a theological power, theological in the deeper and broader sense of coming from God and at work in a variety of ways in the life and history of people. This is evident from our discussion in the previous chapter of how Jesus endeavors to rectify the faith and theology of the official religion of his time. In this chapter we will further explore the nature of theological power in stories.

POLARIZATION OF POWER

Our experience tells us that power is seldom neutral when it manifests itself in our lives and in the histories of nations and the world. When it gets actualized and becomes visible, it is either positive or negative, either constructive or destructive, either right or wrong, either good or evil. Power in its manifestation is thus polarized. What ensues is the conflict between these polarities of power and the struggle to overcome the polarities. What we see and experience in our personal lives and in the life and history outside us is the conflict and struggle between these polarities of power—either good overcoming evil or evil defeating good, for example. A story that revolves around such conflict and struggle, victory and defeat, becomes a drama of life and history, told and retold, enacted and reenacted, one generation after another to remind us of one fundamental fact, namely, the destructive and constructive nature of power. To use the words of Jeremiah the prophet in ancient Judah who heard God call him and say to him:

> Now I have put my words in your mouth.
> See, today I appoint you over
> nations and over kingdoms,
> to pluck up and to pull down,
> to destroy and to overthrow,
> to build and to plant. (Jer 1:9–10)

Is power already polarized in God—the power to destroy and overthrow the nations and to build and plant them? Is this power then injected into our life and the history of the world, causing destruction or construction, victory or defeat, in our life and in the history of the nations?

Or is the polarization of power created by us humans, carried out in our life and in the history of the nations, then projected back onto God, making God responsible for the conflicts of power in our life and in the world? It must be the latter. God has not instituted the polarization of power; it is we humans who have instituted it. God does not create conflicts and discords of power; it is we humans who create them. But the strange thing is that in telling how we humans polarize power and create conflict among us, we also hear the stories of how the saving power of God is at work in our life and in the world. This power of God's saving love, this theological power, is the power of God, working in our life and in our world. God is power, but not just any kind of power. Surely, it is not the power polarized to create conflicts and strife in our life and in the world. God's is the power of the redeeming love that works in all sorts of ways to bring about well-being in us and in human community. And many stories testify to this redeeming power of God's in our life and in the world. How could theology be anything other than stories of testimony to it?

THE LAMENT OF A JAPANESE MOTHER

What is this theological power like? How is it at work in human community reflecting the saving love of God? And what does it do to enable people to perceive light in darkness, regain hope in the midst of despair, and believe in life despite death?

Here is a story told by a Japanese mother, herself a victim of the atomic bomb that devastated the city of Hiroshima and killed tens of thousands of people in an instant on the fateful day of the 6th of August,

1945, the story of the first atomic bomb dropped in Hiroshima, Japan, that ended the tragic and cruel Pacific War in a most tragic and cruel manner. As we read this story, we should picture for ourselves the story-teller and the listeners around her. We must, in our minds' eyes, look at the mother who, though overwhelmed by the tragedy, is dignified and noble as she tells the heartbreaking story. We must also visualize the faces of the listeners completely absorbed in her story, spellbound by her power of telling a shocking story. This is her story:

> Iwojima fell,
> Okinawa fought to the last man—
> not even empty funerary urns came back,
> cities throughout the land were burned to blackened waste,
> and then
> August sixth, 1945:
> blue sky perfectly still.
> Air-raid hood of padded cotton
> over your shoulder,
> you were mobilized to raze buildings
>   for the forced evacuations—
>
> suddenly,
> the blue flash:
> buildings collapse,
> fires blaze,
> and amid swirling smoke
> hordes of people in flight
> thread their way through downed wires.
>
> On the evening of the third day
> we brought your corpse home.
> A dark night: air-raid alarm
> that was never lifted.
> In the black night Hiroshima burned red.
> The eve of the surrender,
> all Japan as if holding vigil.
> A dark room sealed off by blackout curtains.
> You laid out before the *butsudan*,[1]
> a white handkerchief over your face.
> In the dusk at the aid station

1. The translator, Dr. Richard Minear, writes: "A *butsudan* is a Buddhist altar in a private home. Koi was then a suburb of Hiroshima, at the foot of the hills immediately to the west of the city."

crazed victims
had shouted like wild animals
and raced about the classrooms;
grotesquely swollen, people with burns had groaned
and given off alive the stench of death.
The corpses were lined up like so many heaps of rags
on the dirt floor of Koi Primary School,
and we knew you only by your metal ID.
Over your face—
a white handkerchief
someone had placed there.
The handkerchief was stuck fast to your burns
and would not come off.

A junior in girls' higher school,
not understanding what the war was about,
you died, Sachiko, before you could blossom.
Your mother
draped a brand-new gown [*yukata*],
white and flowered,
over the school uniform burned to tatters
and seared onto your skin.
"I made it for you, but because of the war,
you never got to wear it."
Her arms around you, she broke down and wept.

—August 1946[2]

This is a lament of a mother crying her heart out for her daughter disfigured and killed by the atomic bomb. This is a sorrowful song sung by a mother looking for her daughter among the heaps of mutilated lifeless bodies. And this is a heartbreaking story of a mother who had to bury the daughter she nurtured and protected for ten months in her womb.

And yet, what you read here grips you with power. Yes, there is power in this lament; it is the power of a mother's love for her daughter in life and all the more in death. There is power in this sad song; it is the power of words that bind a mother and her daughter not only in life

---

2. "Saichiko, Dead in the Atomic Bombing," pages 182–83 of *Black Eggs: Poems by Kurihara Sadako*, translated with an introduction and notes by Richard H. Minear, Michigan Monograph Series in Japanese Studies, Number 12 (Ann Arbor: Center for Japanese Studies, The University of Michigan, 1994). © 1994 The Regents of the University of Michigan. All rights reserved. Used with the permission of the publisher.

but also in death. There is power in this story; it is the power of life that death has not been able to conquer.

THEOLOGICAL POWER OF STORIES

There are many kinds of power; among them is theological power. Ultimately, power is theological in origin and nature because it is not inherent in human beings, but bestowed on them by God. It is theological because it is not the power of human beings but the power with which God empowers human beings to live, believe, hope and love. And it is theological because it is the power that binds God and human beings in the struggle for a tomorrow without despair, a future without horrendous weapons of mass destruction such as atomic bombs. And it is theological because it is the power that enables human beings to rise from the rubbles of history to envision a life of peace and love with God in the world.

Power of Empathy

As you listen to this lament, this sad song and this heartbreaking story, the face of the Japanese mother with tears streaming down her eyes and the faces of listeners with their eyes filled with tears, move you and overwhelm you. Without being aware of it, you are that mother; you are one of the listeners. The story breaks the barriers that separate you from them; it removes the obstruction that keeps them and you apart. This is the power of empathy. A story transformed into a lament and a song has this power of empathy.

At the end of the Japanes mother's lament, she cries her heart out when she finds her daughter dead in her arms after a frantic search.

> A junior in girls' higher school,
> not understanding what the war was about,
> you died, Sachiko, before you could blossom.
> Your mother
> draped a brand-new gown,
> white and flowered,
> over the school uniform burned to tatters
> and seared onto your skin.
> "I made it for you, but because of the war,
> you never got to wear it."
> Her arms around you, she broke down and wept.

The Japanese mother holding her dead daughter in her arms breaks down in tears. You who hear this lament may also break down in tears. Who could remain unmoved by a story such as this? Who could turn away from it as if it had nothing to do with them? Such is the power of empathy contained in this story.

This lament of a Japanese mother reminds us of Michaelangelo's (1475–1564) *Pieta*, the marble statue showing the mourning Mary, the mother of Jesus, holding the dead Jesus on her knees after his crucifixion. The story of Mary with her dead son on her knees and the story of the Japanese mother holding her dead daughter in her arms—they are two different stories: one took place two thousand years ago in Palestine, the Middle East, the other twenty centuries later in Japan; one was the story of a Jewish mother, the other that of a Japanese mother. But as you listen to the lament of the Korean mother and see the *Pieta*, does not your heart go out to both mothers, even though their circumstances are different in every way?

Your theological discernment perceives nothing common in these two mothers. For Mary it is the crucifixion of her son, the tragic event that was later to develop into the central doctrine of redemption in Christian theology, while the Japanese mother happens to lose her daughter in the atomic bombing. Mary was later to be adored and worshipped as the Virgin Mary in Christian piety, whereas the Japanese mother remains anonymous. But does not your heart go out to both mothers, the mother in the *Pieta* and the mother in the lament? Such is the power of empathy in stories, the power that transcends time and space and the power that eclipses ethnic, cultural even religious differences. Story can achieve this because of its power of empathy, a power that the doctrines and teachings of most religions, including Christianity, does not possess.

Image-Making Power

This power of empathy is what most theological textbooks and treatises do not possess. Theology does not make us *see*, but a story does. A theological thesis does not enable us to *hear*, but a story does. A theological proposition does not *touch* the heart of God and the hearts of human beings gripped by love and agonized by tragedies of life, but story does. Story makes us see deeply into the abyss of the human heart desperately looking for the God of love. It enables us to experience and portray pain and joy in pictures and images. This is the most "primitive" or "primordial" power God bestowed on human beings from the beginning. And how marvelously the creation story in the Hebrew Bible theologizes the image-making power of human beings! It tells us:

> So God created humankind in God's image,
> in the image of God, God created them,
> male and female God created them. (Gen 1:27)

This is a truly marvelous story. That is why we can tell it over and over tirelessly. It will not cease to arouse our curiosity about who we are and who God is. It does not cease to inspire us to venture to the brink of the mystery of communion between God and humanity.

If God created humankind in God's concept, then there will be no such image-making power that draws God and humanity together in tension and in companionship. God is not a bundle of concepts, just as we human beings are not. God is not made up of ideas, and neither are we human beings. Concepts and ideas can be made and discarded in ways that stories cannot. Theology constructed on concepts and ideas can come and go, but theology built on stories last much longer than we can imagine because of their image-making power.

It was therefore a mistake for the Reformation in Europe four hundred years ago, and especially in the city of Geneva in which the Calvinist Reformation flourished, to banish images from the church. This is to throw the baby out with the bathwater. To deny the image-making power of humans is to deny the creation story of God creating, not in God's concept, but in God's image. The power to think in images, to construct images, is a God-given power. This biblical and theological basis of human ability to image things, this innate human faculty to image things, is confused with idolatry; we are enjoined in the second commandment "not to make a carved image nor likeness of anything in the heavens above, or on the earth below, or in the waters under the earth" (Exod 20:4 RNEB). From this confusion Christian missions mounted attacks against idolatry as the number one sin. Consequently, a lot of native and indigenous images of religious and spiritual cultures were destroyed. To this day missionary Christianity in Asia and Africa is still shunned by the majority of people of other religions as an uncompromising iconoclastic religion.

As a matter of fact the most powerful image-makers are stories. Stories are not just words, spoken or written. Stories paint pictures, create images, erect statues, construct a universe of meaning out of the pictures, images and monuments they make with words and sounds. The image created in the Japanese mother's story is powerful, more powerful than the words conveyed in the story. We read in the story, for instance, the following words:

> suddenly,
> the blue flash:
> buildings collapse,
> fires blaze,
> and amid swirling smoke
> hordes of people in flight
> thread their way through downed wires.

Is this not a picture of devastation perpetrated by the first atom bomb ever used by humans? Is this not an image of the horror created by a weapon of mass destruction? And is this not a memorial of the atrocity committed by humans against humans? Story is words with pictures, images, and monuments. It speaks to our souls and spirits, not just to our brain. Are these words of the Japanese mother not more eloquent than much rhetoric against war? Are they not more powerful than any weapon? They are more eloquent and powerful because they paint pictures of horror, create images of atrocity, and erect monuments over the ruins of human civilization.

The Power of Communion

Stories arise out of a community of women, men and children, are told and handed down in community, and create a common destiny of people in the community. It is a communion of people drawn together by the stories they share. Story has this power of communion-making and communion-building. It creates a bond of kinship that goes beyond blood kinship. There is a Chinese saying that "blood is thicker than water" (*shiueh nong yu shoei* in Chinese). It can also be paraphrased to say, "story is more dense than blood relationship."

The power of stories is active in human community. It may change people's hearts and minds and transform their social, political and spiritual commitment and loyalty. How are we to understand such power of stories? How are we to come to grips with it? It does not help to theorize about such questions. A story is to be told and not to be theorized. It is to be absorbed by our souls in its totality and not to be dissected into parts. Stories are to be shared as widely as possible, and not to be kept as something that belongs only to those who possess power and privilege, those who could do anything they like. That is why stories can often be the matrix of social change, political revolution, even religious transformation. When you feel this power of a story in your being, a story can empower you to become not a passive spectator but an active participant in the building of a new community.

What kind of communion emerges out of people knit together by stories? It is a communion of the storyteller and listeners. It is the communion of women, men and children. A communion of the young and the old. It is the communion of the living and the dead within the spiritual universe of God's creation. Storytelling is therefore cosmic in nature; it is a cosmic act involving humans and God, humans seeking the meaning of life and history and God enabling humans to perceive the meaning of meanings, that is, the divine meaning that makes sense of human meaning on the one hand and transcends meaninglessness on the other.

This reminds us of the Last Supper Jesus had with his followers before his crucifixion. According to Mark, the author of the earliest Gospel, Jesus

> took a loaf of bread and after blessing it broke it, gave it to them, and said, "Take, this is my body." Then he took a cup, and after giving thanks he gave it to them, and all of them drank from it. He said to them, "This is my blood of the covenant, which is poured out for many . . ." (Mark 14:22–25)

This story is a communion story, a communion created by Jesus and his followers as they ate from the same loaf of bread and drank from the same cup of wine. That the Last Supper has come to be called "communion" is not accidental. It is the communion that anticipates the death of Jesus and the communion of envisioning life together through his death. It is a communion of life through death. The Lord's Supper the Christian church celebrates in the past and today is not just to remember what happened to Jesus a long time ago, merely a ritual to remind ourselves of what Jesus had to go through two thousand years ago. What it does is to re-create communion between Jesus and those who are gathered in the communion of life through his death.

In stories is embedded this power of communion. It is not something added to it from outside. Stories are born with that power. That power of communion is inherent in stories. Stories without that power do not endure. Such stories do not get etched in human memory. They are told to be forgotten. They sink into oblivion. But the story of the Japanese mother is not told to be forgotten. It does not fade into oblivion. It creates a communion of life in people, a communion of the living and the dead, even though what it recounts is a story of tragic death.

That is why the story moves back and forth from the first person singular to the first person plural. It breaks through the boundary of I and them to create a communion of we. In it I am We and We are I. When death occurs, it is not just some individual who dies; something in us all dies. That something is called death. And when life is born, it is not just some individual who is born; something in us all comes into being. That something is called life. This is the communion-making power of stories. The Apostle Paul is right when he explains the meaning of baptism to the Christians at Rome: ". . . we have been buried with him [Jesus] by baptism into death, so that, just as Christ was raised from the dead by the glory of the Father, so we too might walk in newness of life" (Rom 6:4).

The communion of "we" develops in the midst of the horrible death for which the first atomic bomb was responsible. The frantic search for the daughter is not carried out by the mother alone, but by "we."

> The corpses were lined up like so many heaps of rags
> on the dirt floor of Koi Primary School,
> and we knew you only by your metal ID.

Who are these "we"? They are the men and women terrified and wounded by the atomic bomb, the weapon of mass murder. They are people desperately looking for life in the midst of death.

They are from different walks of life, engaged in different professions, pursing different interests. But now all these differences have disappeared. They are united in a communion bond of one supreme purpose of living instead of dying. All their differences disappear because of this supreme effort to live not only their own lives but the lives of others. This is a sacred communion, most basic and deepest communion, a communion that emerged as Jesus sat down with his followers for the last time to give them the bread and wine of life in face of his imminent death. That is why when we celebrate the Lord's Supper to remember that last supper, we call it "the holy communion." The communion is holy because the life on which Jesus' last supper and our Lord's Supper are focused is holy.

Power in Suffering

In this holy communion, be it the communion in search of Sachiko, the young Japanese schoolgirl, or the communion that enveloped Jesus and his followers at the Last Supper, we not only witness but are moved by the power of suffering. Who wants to suffer? Who wants to undergo physical suffering? Physical suffering is ugly; it disfigures and destroys one's humanity, the humanity of not only the victims but also the victim-izers. It inevitably leads to spiritual suffering. This is poignantly true in the case of torture. This is the whole point: torture deprives the victims of their humanity, rendering them as less than human. At the same time, unbeknownst to themselves, those who inflict torture on others also de-prive themselves of their humanity.

But there are cases in which suffering becomes a source of power. What is that power of suffering? It is the power to defy suffering, the power not to yield to it, the power to remain human in the face of in-humanity. At least it is the power to preserve sanity that suffering may destroy. The Japanese mother and her friends are on the verge of in-sanity. The suffering of their seriously maimed bodies, the fear of their own death and the premonition about the death of the little girl they are looking for, make them almost insane. This is the negative power of suffering.

But there is a positive power of suffering, the power that enables them to live in spite of threat of death, the power that seeks the living in the midst of the dead. This is a spiritual power. We recall the women at Jesus' tomb grieving his death on the cross. It has, however, suddenly dawned on them: "Why do we look for the living among the dead?" (Luke 24:5) This is the positive power of suffering, the power to look for the living when death is all around, the power to continue believing in life when death has done its work, and the power to hope in the midst of the despair created by death.

It is this power of suffering that fills the story of the Japanese mother and those who seek the little girl with the mother. Let us listen to the story once again. Their frantic search takes them to a public school where the little daughter of the Japanese mother was enrolled. What they see is

> grotesquely swollen, people with burns had groaned
> and given off alive the stench of death.
> The corpses were lined up like so many heaps of rags
> on the dirt floor of Koi Primary School,
> and we knew you only by your metal ID.
> Over your face—
> a white handkerchief
> someone had placed there.
> The handkerchief was stuck fast to your burns
> and would not come off.

This is a picture of hell, of horrendous human suffering and a human tragedy of abysmal dimensions. In face of the suffering of such magnitude, life has no meaning. What reigns is death, the sinister face of death, the sardonic laughter of death.

Can one still speak of power in such suffering? Does it make sense to look for power in it? Yes, one must discover power in suffering, and if one cannot discover it, one has to create it. If we are not to yield to the savage force of suffering that human beings inflict on each other, we must believe in the power that can overcome suffering, defying it and creating a new beginning out of it.

The Power of Love

What is this power—the power that can defy, overcome and make a new beginning out of suffering? It is the power of love. Let us listen to the Japanese mother once again:

> Your mother
> draped a brand-new gown [*yukata*],
> white and flowered,
> over the school uniform burned to tatters
> and seared onto your skin.
> "I made it for you, but because of the war,
> you never got to wear it."
> Her arms around you, she broke down and wept.

A *yukata* is a bath robe Japanese people relax in after they have taken a bath in the evening. The Japanese mother hand-made one for her daughter. Every stitch was made with love. Her daughter would have reminded herself of her mother's love for her every evening she came home and put it on after taking a bath. But that *yukata* is now used as a shroud over her on top of "the tattered uniform seared permanently to her skin."

Is this the end of the tragedy? Is this the last rite the Japanese mother could do for her daughter who died all too prematurely? Does she now have to turn her daughter over to death, to eternal oblivion? But there is something else she can do. She is not going to give up her daughter to death easily. The bond of love between her and her daughter is so strong that even death could not sever it. Prompted by her love for her daughter,

> Her arms around you, she broke down and wept.

A mother holding in her arms the body of her daughter that "looked like heaps of tattered rags." She does not shrink back in fear; instead she holds in her arms her daughter turned into "heaps of tattered rags." She does not recoil in horror, but holds her daughter close to her heart, lying lifeless "on the dirt floor of the makeshift morgue."

This is what only a mother can do, a mother who nurtured her daughter for ten months in her womb, who responded to every sign of her growing life with joy and in expectation. This love is too great and too deep for death to take away. This is almost a divine kind of love. It reminds us once again of Michaelangelo's *Pieta*. Whether looking at Mary holding the lifeless Jesus on her lap or the Japanese mother holding her dead daughter in her arms, what comes to one's mind are the Apostle Paul's words of unsurpassable beauty and profundity in his letter to the Christians at Rome:

> For I am convinced that neither death, nor life, nor angels, nor rulers, nor things present, nor things to come, nor powers, nor height, nor depth, nor anything else in all creation, will be able to separate us from the love of God in Christ Jesus our Lord. (Rom 8:38–39)

This must be the love manifested in the Japanese mother who firmly holds the lifeless body of her daughter in her arms.

The story of the Japanese mother is the story of love; it is the story in which the power of love is at work. The word "love" is not used in the entire story, not even once. But it is love that moves us in the story. The story moves us because it is the story of the power of love that triumphs over the power of death.

The Power of Transcendence

This power of love in stores is the power of transcendence. As we have seen in the Japanese mother's story, that power of love transcends over the power of death. It enables us to envision life beyond death.

This power of transcendence manifests itself in more than one way. If it is the power of life over death, it is because it is the power that brings *illo tempore*, that "great time," that time outside time and beyond time, to the present time and even to the future time. It is the power that breaks the barriers of time, making the past live today and tomorrow. A story can possess that power of transcendence. It is not told to disappear into thin air, leaving no trace in our memory. Once told, a story runs in the veins of the people, is stored in the memory of a community, and re-membered in the history of a nation.

What moves us in a story such as the Japanese mother's or the story carved in the *Pieta* is a strong power, exerting profound effects on us. It creates consciousness that fortifies ethnic identity. It nurtures an ethos that becomes embodied in the culture of a people. That power in stories is a power of hope in the future, not a future that could only be envisioned but not real in the present, but a future that could be lived in the present. It is the power of resurrection, the power that renews time and creates life. This power of transcendence in stories is a theological power, the power of God at work in human beings.

We cannot, therefore, but wonder whether it is God who has planted that power of transcendence, that power to transcend time with eternity, despair with hope, desperation with faith, and death with life. That is why a story takes us to the present and the future by taking us back to the past. That is why it inspires new stories to be added to the well of stories, new voices to be uttered in the midst of old voices, and new dreams to dream when a dream gets old and loses its power.

Is it not this power of the story that prompts Mary to sing the Magnificat? The Magnficat is a song; it is a hymn; it is a painting, and above all it is a story:

> My soul magnifies the Lord,
> and my spirit rejoices in God my Savior,
> for he has looked with favor on
> the lowliness of his servant.
> Surely, from now on
> all generations will call me blessed,
> for the Mighty One has done great things for me,

and holy is his name.
His mercy is for those who fear him
From generation to generation . . . (Luke 1:46–55)

Ever since Mary told the story of the Magnificat two thousand years ago, it has not ceased to be told again and again. It is told today and it will be told in the future.

I do not know whether the Japanese mother knew the Magnificat. If she did, she would have been inspired to tell the story of the Magnificat. The Magnificat was her story too, just as it was the story of Mary, the mother of Jesus, the story of the generations of women and men who live in the shadow of oppression and death. Telling stories can therefore be an act of healing both physical pain and spiritual anguish. In stories is the divine power of transcendence made flesh and lived among us.

6

In Search of Our Roots

IN 1977 ALEX HALEY, the African-American writer, published a monumental story titled *Roots*, with the subtitle, "The Epic Drama of One Man's Search for His Origins." His dedication to the book reads:

> It wasn't planned that *Roots'* researching and writing finally would take twelve years. Just by chance it is being published in the Bicentennial Year of the United States.
>
> So I dedicate *Roots* as a birthday offering to my country within which most of *Roots* happened.

Roots is not just "one man's search for his origins"; it is African-Americans' search for their origins, the search of the people of the United States for their origins. Furthermore, it is humanity's search for their origins. In his acknowledgments Alex Haley expresses his deep gratitude to "so many people for their help with Roots that pages would be required simply to list them all."

Alex Haley begins the search for his roots in this way: "Early in the spring of 1750, in the village of Juffure, four days upriver from the coast of The Gambia, West Africa, a man-child was born to Omoro and Binta Kinte . . ."[1] As the story unfoldeds, we realize that the birth of a baby boy was not a common-place story. Every birth, boy or girl, female or male, is an extraordinary story. At the naming ceremony of the baby boy on the eighth day of his birth, Omoro, the father, "carrying little Kunta in his strong arms, walked to the edge of the village, lifted his baby up with

---

1. Haley, *Roots*, v.

his face to the heavens, and said softly, *'fend killing dorong leh warrata ka iteh tee'* (Behold, the only thing greater than yourself)."[2]

WHAT IS STORY?

The search for one's roots begins with an individual, but it is not merely an individual story. As the story of *Roots* meanders its way through Kunta's destiny with complex and tortuous twists and turns, it expands from one individual to the family and to the entire clan; it extends from a small village in Africa to the raging seas and to the new continent of America, involving not just one people and one nation but many peoples and many nations. Finally, it stretches out to include the whole of humanity.

Neither is *Roots* just the story of Kunta nor merely the story of Alex Haley; it is the story of every American. Even more, it is the story of you and me, a story of humanity. That is why you and I, who are outsiders to the story, can resonate with it, live it and become part of its journey from darkness to light, from despair to hope, and from death to life. A story such as this has, as we have seen, such a compelling power of empathy, compassion, communion and transcendence. We must, therefore, explore further in this chapter the nature of stories as the search for our roots, the search that takes us to all dimensions of our life, physical and spiritual, to all layers of meaning, human and divine, and to all aspects of time within our temporality and the divine assurance of eternity. What we are going to do in this chapter is to probe the question of what constitutes the roots of stories.

STORIES ARE HUMAN SEARCH FOR LOVE

Love is the fountain of life; life is originated in it and comes into being from it. Love is the essence of life; without it, life might have a form but would have no substance. Love is the seed of life; life is conceived in it, grown in it and fulfilled in it. Love, to sum up, is the root of life; life without it, just as a tree without roots, would wither, fade away and die.

Although love is so essential to life, it is not there ready to be at our service, not to mention at our disposal. Love can turn into a brutal force that simply sustains the physical needs of an organism, but the love that has turned into a brute physical force is not love. It is a naked force that

2. Ibid., 3.

completely suppresses that which makes love a deep spiritual experience mediated through physical experience. That is why stories as the search for human roots have to be stories of the love that actualizes spiritual dimensions deeply embedded in human nature.

Stories, first and foremost, are, therefore, stories of love. This has been true since time immemorial to the present time, in the East or West, South or North. Is not the search for love immortalized in literature, painting, sculpture, music? Is it not the principal motif of operas, plays and dances on the stage and on the movie or television screens? The main theme that runs through all sacred scriptures is also love. And does not love often turn the stories of pain and joy, despair and hope, death and life in our ordinary daily life into extraordinary dramas, heartrending tragedies or wonderful comedies?

The Story of Spring Fragrance

Love as the life force that brings forth life and ennobles human nature to rise above the adversities of life and to seek justice in society is the theme of the story of "Spring Fragrance," a most popular story in Korea throughout its history. It has played countless times on the stage and on the movie screen in a variety of versions. The story has a legendary character. Legend or not, it is a story that happens to people who struggle to live in a world in which to be true to love demands courage and human dignity.

There is of course romance in the story; essentially it is a story of the heart. Is not love an affair of the heart? There are tears in the story, helpless tears shed by those at the mercy of the powerful. But love does not mean leaving every thing, even one's life, to fate. The love of the weak turns into rage in the story, rage against the moral degradation of those in power.

The story of the woman called Spring Fragrance is the story of the search for human moral roots in love. It is a long story filled with suspense at every turn. "Formerly there lived in the Province of Cholla in the town of Nawwon a magistrate who had a son named Yi Doryung," begins the story. It so happens that one morning Yi Doryung was at a summer pavilion near a bridge called "Ojak-kyo" or the "Magpie Bridge" to see wildflowers, when

> he caught sight of a young maiden swinging, suspended from
> the branches of a tree. . . . the maiden was named Choon Hyang

(Spring Fragrance), a daughter of Wolmai (Moon Plum), the re-
tired *kisaeng* . . . She was very pretty, the wind blowing back her
hair with its long ribbon over her rosy face . . .

[In the meantime] Choon Hyang's mother had a dream in
which a blue dragon coiled itself round Choon Hyang's body and
finally holding her in its mouth, flew up to the sky. Looking up,
instead of the dragon in the clouds, she saw a dragon on earth,
for Yi Doryung, that is Yi Mongyang ("Dream-Dragon"), came
and spoke to her. On learning the purpose of his visit she called
Choon Hyang to meet the young nobleman and Yi Doryung
asked Choon Hyang's mother for the hand of her daughter. The
old woman thinking her dream had come true, gladly consented
but said: "You are a nobleman's son and Choon Hyang is a daughter of the people, so there cannot be a formal marriage, but if you
give us a secret marriage certificate, writing your pledge not to
desert her, we shall be contented."

Yi Doryung seized a pen and set down the following lines:
"The blue sea may become a mulberry field, and the mulberry
field may become the blue sea but my heart for Choon Hyang
shall not change. Heaven and earth and all gods are witnesses."

This is what is called "*hai shi shan meng*" in Chinese, meaning "vow of
eternal love," the vow a man and a woman make to each other when they
fall in love with each other. For Yi Doryung and Choon Hyang the test of
the vow of eternal love to each other has just begun. To Yi Doryung's dis-
may he has to accompany his father back to Seoul, the capital, where his
father is to join the king's cabinet. Then the story depicts a most touching scene of Yi Doryung taking "a most tender leave of Choon Hyang
parting with Choon Hyang" who saw him off at the Magpie Bridge.

> "Since there is no help, let us embrace and part," said Choonhyang,
> throwing her hands around her lover's neck. Then she gives her
> ring to him, saying: "This is my token of love for you. Keep it
> until we meet again. Go in peace, but do not forget me. I shall
> remain faithful to you and wait here till we come and take me
> away to Seoul."

But fate seems to play a cruel trick on Yi Doryung and Choon Hyang.
After Yi Doryung's departure a new magistrate arrived in Namwon.
He was a despot, treating people like grass, attaching no importance to
human life. He was enraged when his approach to Choon Hyang was
rejected and had her put in prison. Not to be daunted, she protested and
said: "Why put me in prison? I have done no wrong. A married woman
must be faithful to her husband. If the King was replaced by a usurper,

would you serve the upstart monarch?" The Magistrate was furious and ordered her to be executed.

In the meantime Yi Doryung, appointed Usa (His Majesty's Royal Envoy), arrived in Namwon disguised as a beggar to find out how people were faring under the new Magistrate. He composed a poem to express what he had seen in Namwon:

> The beautiful wine in golden vases
> Is the blood of a thousand people.
> This magnificent meat on these jade tables
> Is the flesh and marrow of ten thousand lives.
> When the drops roll down from the candles,
> Burning in this banquet hall,
> The tears of the hungry people
> Pour from their sunken eyes.
> Even louder than the noisy song of these courtesans
> Resound the complaints of the oppressed peasants.

This is a call to rise against the despotic Magistrate. Terribly frightened, the Magistrate and his officials fled the government offices in panic.

Yi Doryung, the King's envoy, now sitting in the Magistrate's seat, had Choon Hyang brought to his court. He addressed Choon Hyang in these stern words to test her faithfulness to him:

> "If you do not love the Magistrate, will you love me and come to me, the King's Envoy? If you refuse, I shall order my men to strike off your head immediately."

Not recognizing the King's Envoy to be Yi Doryung, her husband, "Alas!" exclaimed Choon Hyang,

> "How unhappy are the poor people of this country! First the in-justice of the Magistrate, then you, the Envoy of the King, who should help and protect the unhappy people, you think imme-diately to condemn to death a poor girl whom you desire. O we people are poor; women are weak and sad."
>
> Yi Doryung then order the courtesans to untie the cords which bound the hands of Choon Hyang [and said to her]: "Now raise your head and look at me."
>
> "No," she answered, "I shall not look at you, I shall not listen to you. Cut my body into pieces if you like, but I shall never go to you." Yi Doryung was delighted. He took off his ring and ordered a courtesan to show it to Choon Hyang. She saw that it was the one she had given to Yi Doryung, and lifting her yes, recognized her lover . . .

>Yi Doryung ordered a sedan chair to be brought at once and saw that Choon Hyang was safely carried to her home. The People shouted with joy and gave cheers for Choon Hyang and Yi Doryung. . . .

Love is never a straightforward affair. This story proves that. Love is a tortuous road, but to be true to love as the root of life and destiny, how could love not be a journey filled with thorns and thistles? And this is how love's mettle is tested. Love that cannot stand tests is false love, pretentious love, the love that yields to seduction of power, position, and wealth. It is the love that betrays the very roots of human nature. Both Yi Doryung and Choon Hyang have stood the tests that seek to disrupt and even destroy the bond of love that formed between them.

But love as search for human roots goes beyond the bond that binds a man and a women in love. Love as the root of human nature is demonstrated in the sense of justice for society and people. The poem composed by Yi Doryung bristles with the injustice people suffered under the cruel Magistrate. His love for the suffering people turned into bitter rage against the oppressive ruler. It awakened the people from their fatalism and drove the vicious ruler and his cronies from their seat of oppression.

As to Choonhyang, the nobleness of her love turns into defiance against the degenerate Magistrate when the latter tries to take advantage of her. But her defiance is not merely a matter of maintaining her unchangeable love for her husband and keeping her integrity as a human being. Bound and taken to the Magistrate for trial, she becomes a voice for the voiceless. Undaunted, she addresses herself to the Magistrate, declaring: "The King has sent you to Namwon to take care of the people. . . . you had better fulfill your duties and apply justice according to the law of the country."

When taken to the King's Envoy, she did not recognize him to be her husband, Yi Doryung. Thinking that he was no better than the former Magistrate, she spoke out for the people who had long been reduced to silence: "Alas! How unhappy are the people of this country! First the injustice of the Magistrate, then you, the Envoy of the King, who should help and protect the unhappy people—you think immediately to condemn a poor girl whom you desire. O we people are poor; women are weak and sad."

What you see in this woman is love inflamed by defiance against unjust political power, love inflamed by the fate of the poor people, including herself. Is this not liberation theology before the liberation theology of Latin America in the twentieth century? Is this not a women's movement long before the women's movements developed in the West in the last two centuries? What we have in the story of "Spring Fragrance" is liberation theology at its best and a women's movement at its deepest. The heart of this liberation theology and this women's movement is love, love in search of human roots.

STORIES ARE HUMAN QUESTS FOR HOPE

Life is born in hope, hope for growth and development. Life is lived in hope, hope for a better future and fulfillment. And life faces death in hope, the hope that death is not the end of life but the beginning of a new life. If love is the force that gives birth to life, hope gives meaning and purpose to life. Stories of love are thus stories of hope, stories of why the human search for the roots of life is a never-ending adventure carried out from one generation to the next.

Hope, as a matter of fact, is not a rare commodity; it is an everyday happening. It is the hope of being united with loved ones that enables the inmates of concentration camps to endure the brutality of their captors and the hardships of their prison life. It is the hope for a cure that inspires terminally ill patients to embrace their pain and suffering. It is the hope for young people to make good or fail, to raise their heads above the sky (*chhut thau thi*), as the people in Taiwan would say. It inspires many immigrant parents in America to work day and night for their children. Without hope a person would grow old prematurely and die, a society would be at the mercy of lawlessness and wrecked by moral depravity, and a nation would be a prey to another nation. Humanity is rooted in hope as much as in love.

The Story of Two Suns

That is why stories of hope abound. They come in all forms and shapes, are painted in all colors and all shades of colors, and are told in all languages and cultures. Here is a typical "hope story" that never ceases to fascinate the Atayal people of Taiwan, one of the eleven tribes that had come from the South Pacific to inhabit the island many centuries before. It is the story of how some tribal warriors in ancient times and their descendants conquered two suns to bring peace and prosperity to their tribe. Here is the story:

> Once upon a time there were two suns in the sky. When one sun set in the west, the other sun rose in the east, and there was no night on earth. The strong heat from the suns dried up all rivers. Fishes could not live, grass and trees died, birds and animals were not able to survive. Human beings became restless. They could not find food, lived in misery and suffered in the extreme. Everyone knew that unless one of the suns was shot down, in no time they would all die. The village elders held a council in which they decided to send out three robust young warriors on an expedition to shoot down one of the suns. This was not going to be an easy task because the suns were so high and far away . . .
>
> The three young warriors, besides equipping themselves with bows, arrows, sharp daggers, each had his newborn baby strapped on the back. They also took with them a lot of tangerine and millet seeds. As they went forward, they planted the seeds on the ground. . . .
>
> Several decades passed, but they were not any nearer the suns. They grew old and died one by one. In the meantime the babies carried by their fathers on the expedition became adults. It was now their turn to carry out the mission. At last they arrived at their destination. Seeing the red suns hung low on the edge of the sky, they took aim at the suns, and after a few failed attempts, finally succeeded in shooting right through the middle of one of the suns. At this the heaven shook and the earth moved, and with horrendous sounds the bloody sun fell from the sky, and struck one of the warriors dead.
>
> The fiery sun, now a pale and cold carcass, having lost all its brilliant rays, is called the moon. The stars are the stains of the blood from the sun shot down by the warriors. From that time on, there was day and night on earth. People were able to sleep when it was night. All things under the sun were able to live again, thriving and prospering.
>
> With the mission accomplished, the two warriors set out on their journey back home. The return journey did not seem as long as the previous journey. And to their joy, the seeds their fathers had sown on their outward journey now grew into trees bearing abundant fruits and grains, giving them food and nourishment. When they reached home and told them what they had done, they were welcomed home with open arms and banquets . . . [3]

3. Abridged and translated from Chinese into English by the author from Lin Dao-Sheng, *Collection of Myths and Stories of Aborigines*, 21–23.

What a rich story of hope! How are we to penetrate the depths of its meaning and fathom its wisdom? Let us come to grips with it from the most obvious to the least obvious.

First of all, this is an etiological story. It is told to explain why there is one sun, one moon and numerous stars in the sky, why there are day and night, why things grow, why there are sowing times and harvest times, and why life goes on uninterrupted. But to maintain the harmonious relation between living beings and nature does not happen automatically. To achieve it enormous cost has to be paid and huge sacrifices have to be made.

This leads to the second point of the story. It can be summed up in a popular saying in Chinese: *jen ting sheng tien*, meaning "human determination will conquer nature," or "the human being is the master of their own fate." Today this sounds anti-ecological, human beings pitted against nature intent on subduing it. Traditional Christian theology that has human beings at the center or at the pinnacle of God's creation has rendered theological justification for human conquest of nature. We now know this is a wrong theology, a distortion of creation developed on the basis of human centrism.

But the nature with which the aboriginal people of Taiwan lived was not always friendly and hospitable; sometimes it could become unfavorable to their well-being. In this story the adversities of life are caused by the two red-hot suns in the sky, scorching to death everything on earth and threatening them with extinction with merciless heat. They decided that they could not just sit there waiting for doomsday to arrive.

And act they did. The story moves on to the main stage when an audacious plan to shoot down one of the two suns was proposed. The hope was to create a nature regulated by day and night, four seasons, work in the daytime and sleep in the nighttime. The plot thickened as the three young warriors were chosen to carry out the plan; thus began the dangerous expedition to where the suns were. Since it was going to be a long and arduous journey from which they would not expect to return alive, they took with them their newborn babies to carry on their efforts after their death. They also took plenty of seeds with them to plant on their way. As expected, it was their sons who accomplished the impossible mission to tame hostile nature and bring well-being to their people.

The story is a story of hope not only for the Atayal people of Taiwan but for all living beings. It is the hope on which all lives depend to live, prosper and continue. Nature is not always kind and hospitable to living beings on earth, including human beings. Sometimes human beings must adjust themselves to nature to live well; after all, human beings are part of nature. But nature sometimes can be unfriendly and inhospitable to living beings. Human beings need to engage nature in creating friendly and beneficial relations for the well-being and prosperity of all those who share it.

The story thus portrays human beings striving to preserve the roots of life extending from past generations, through the present generation, to future generations. No generation of human beings can live by itself and for itself. The present generation owes their lives to their ancestors and they are duty bound to transmit the ancestral life to their posterity. This is one of the ways to ensure that the temporal life is not temporal, but part of immortal life. The hope of the present life is rooted in faith in immortality and in action to ensure it.

This longing for the life that spans eternity is also symbolized in the story by having the three warriors plant seeds of corn and fruit trees along the way. What these three warriors did is to plant the seeds of hope not only for their own lives but for the lives of their children for generations to come. Planting seeds in the ground is an act of hope. Some seeds may die, but there will be seeds that bud, growing roots of life under the ground and bearing fruit above it.

STORIES ARE QUESTS FOR FAITH

In stories people are engaged in search of love and hope. But our experience tells us that love and hope are not ready-made. On the contrary, people suffer because they love and hope. It is safe to say that people who do not suffer, either physically or spiritually, do not know what it is to love and hope. Love without suffering is indulgence and hope without pain is fantasy. For the great majority of us, however, love is not indulgence and hope is not hallucination. What makes life real is the love that suffers and the hope that comes with pain.

The Story of Barbar Deva

But there has to be something that enables us to love in spite of betrayal and inspires us to hope in the midst of adversities. It is faith, or the power of faith in love and hope despite what proves to be the contrary. Here is a story from India, partly historical and partly legendary, a story of faith in the up-hill struggle of the people of India against British colonialism. It is a story of how an outlaw called Barbar Deva, thanks to a social worker who believed in love and nurtured hope for his colonized nation, turned from a bandit feared by the people into a rebel against British rule.

> Once a social worker of the Borsad Chhavani in Gujara [India] was moving from village to village in the area to strengthen the morale of the people against the British government. The people had launched a movement known as the Kheda Satyagraha [love-power] in 1923, and the social worker in the movement was urging the people not to pay any revenue to British officers in cash or kind, as the British officers were taking possession of the land, cattle, household things, etc., and auctioning them, and the farmers were made poor in no time . . .
>
> Barbar Deva, the outlaw, was also harassing the people of the area by looting and plundering them. He was extorting money and kidnapping persons . . .
>
> One night this social worker was passing by a village. . . . In spite of having full knowledge of the menace of the outlaw, he left the village at night for another village, but on his way he met Barbar Deva.
>
> Barbar Deva accosted him and threatened the social worker: "Oh, who are you?"
>
> "I am an outlaw," the social worker replied.
>
> "An outlaw? How can it be? Barbar Deva is the only outlaw of this area."
>
> "I am another one."
>
> "Another one?" He shook his head and said, "I do not know about it. Never . . . no . . . never!"
>
> "Do you doubt my honesty?"
>
> "No, but you have created questions in my mind."
>
> "Well, let us sit and discuss the problem in all its aspects." . . .
>
> And they sat together, and then the social worker began to talk.
>
> "Barbarghai, I am an outlaw against the British government. We outlaws will never harass the poor, meek, and innocent people

as you do. Even though we fight against the British government, we never hide anything from the government. We ourselves give information regarding our strategy to the police department of the government."

"How can it be?" . . .

Barbar Deva was put into a thoughtful mood as soon as he heard the social worker.

Again the worker started talking: "Barbarghai, we are wedded to the cause of truth, and our *gurus* are Mahatma Gandhi and Vallabhaghai Patel."

"They have asked you to practice truth in outlawry?"

"Not only truth, but also nonviolence."

"Double-edged sword you use."

"But the British government dislikes you."

"Me?"

"Yes, it is of no use to harass poor people, innocent traders, and hard-working laborers."

"Oh, I see."

"Also the tiller of the soil."

"I follow you. My good brother, I shall try my best to put your words of advice into practice."

"May the Almighty lead you on the right path."

The social worker blessed him and left for the next village, leaving Barbar Deva in a pensive mood.

After a few days a letter was received in the Borsad Chhavani, addressed to Mahatma Gandhi and Sardar Patel. It was from this outlaw, saying he would be his own, for he was unable to practice nonviolence. He further wrote that when any news that any white officer in the district had been shot dead, they were to understand that it had been done only by Barbar Deva. And thus he would prove himself an outlaw against the British government. He again confessed that he was quite unable to put nonviolence into practice.

It was said that the letter was read by Sardar Patel and was sent to Mahatma Gandhi. The letter was forwarded to the highest authority of the state for the security measures to be taken for the white officers in the district, demanding that Barbar Deva should not be victimized because of his determination.[4]

The story belongs to what is called "unofficial" history of India's struggle against British rule in contrast to "official" history. Although many a story may be "unofficial," they are often more credible and trustworthy

4. "Barbar Deva the Outlaw," in Dorson, *Folktales Told around the World*, 203–5.

than "official" stories. This is especially the case in a society under totalitarian regime or colonial rule.

As is well known, India, under the leadership of Mahatma Gandhi, won independence from the British in 1947, relying on *satyagraha*, meaning truth-force or love-force (*satya* is truth, which equals love, and *graha* is firmness or force),[5] through *ahimsa* (non-violence). Resisting the powerful British Empire with truth-force and love-force by practicing non-violence? Is this not an illusion of the powerless? Is this not a fantasy generated from political naivety? But there were not only leaders such as Gandhi but people such as the social worker in the story who believed in *satyagraha* and practiced *ahimsa*. Together they succeeded in wresting their people and nation from the powerful grips of the British Empire.

The story of the social worker and Babar Deva is a story of faith. Instead of being afraid of Babar Deva, a ruthless outlaw, and against the advice of the well-meaning villagers, the social worker went on his journey, knowing full well that he might meet Babar Deva. What prompted him to do what seemed to be foolish and reckless to the villagers? Was it obstinacy? Was it mere bravado? No, it was faith rooted in hope and love.

The social worker, just as Gandhi, believed that love-force is more powerful than the weapons of violence wielded by British soldiers. They also believed that their longing for independence had far more truth than the truth represented by British colonial rule. As a matter of fact, the colonial rule that demanded the people of India to be subservient was an insult to their humanity. This brings the confrontation of the social worker to the depth of the search of what it means to live under British rule, outlaw or not.

And that makes the conversation between the social worker and the outlaw very fascinating. Straightaway the social worker puts himself on the same level by telling Barba Deva that he too is an outlaw. This is the genius of the story. That arouses the interest and curiosity of Barba Deva. Then the social worker goes on to explain what kind of outlaw he is: an outlaw against the British colonial government, working hard to bring about India's independence, and not an outlaw terrorizing the poor men and women of a small village. The conversation results in a profound effect on Barba Deva, the outlaw. He too gets

5. See Fischer, *Life of Mahatma Gandhi*, 77.

converted to an outlaw against the British government, only that he would carry out his resistance in his own way, not necessarily practicing *satyagraha* and *ahimsa*.

And there is Mahatama Gandhi, the towering figure who brought independence to India through *satyagraha* and *ahimsa*. He is mentioned only once in the story towards the end, but he is present in every line of it and jumps out of every word of it. The story is the story of the social worker and Barba Deva, the outlaw, but it is more than that. It is also about Mahatma Gandhi and his faith in truth-force and love-force. The story is also much more than Gandhi. It is the story of India and its people, the story of how their impossible mission of independence, their struggle to regain their humanity, has been achieved through the faith, hope and love in their future destiny as a liberated nation from a foreign rule.

Gandhi is present in the story even through his conspicuous absence. What manner of man is he, a small, frail-looking man going about barefooted? In this frail frame is an indistinguishable passion for his nation. Aflame in this ascetic body is the faith rooted in *satyagraha* and *ahimsa*, an indomitable spirit of a man whose faith in the victory of truth-force and love-force never flagged. In 1947 the mighty British Empire was on its knees before this ascetic and relinquished its almost two centuries of rule and domination.

Do you see the depth and breadth of this story? From the story of the social worker and the outlaw, a commonplace story, it expands into the story of Mahatma Gandhi and India. But the story does not stop there. The story crosses the oceans and continents to Germany and become the story of Dietrich Bonhoeffer inspired by Gandhi to wage resistance against the demonic Hitler, the Nazi ruler. It also traverses the oceans and continents to reach the shore of North America and become the story of Martin Luther King who led his people in the Civil Rights movement with the same faith, hope and love in *satyagraha* and *ahimsa*. You see, stories such as this have legs to run and the spiritual power to affect people who are entirely foreign to it. Does not this make the reading of stories a spiritual experience?

The story inspires us to know how Gandhi elaborated on *satyagraha* and *ahimsa* and how he practiced them. This is what he said in 1924 as he presented himself to the people of India:

> It is not my intention to suggest that every Englishman or English officer is a devil. Every officer, however, works as part of a Satanic machine and, therefore, whether intentionally or unintentionally, becomes an instrument of injustice, deception and repression. If, holding this belief, I were to conceal it, I would be betraying truth. It is not bad manners to call a thief a thief or a sinner a sinner. . . . On the contrary, if the words have been uttered with sincerity, they can be an expression of love.[6]

This, to quote the Apostle Paul, is "speaking truth in love" (Eph 5:15). How difficult it is not only for the Apostle Paul but also for Gandhi!

What is required of Gandhi is faith as he tries to put speaking truth in love into practice. And here he has to confess it is faith rooted in truth and love that enables him, a Hindu, to transcend religious boundaries. In his own words:

> When Jesus described his times as a generation of vipers, it was not out of anger. At a time when everyone was afraid of telling the truth, Jesus risked his life, described hypocrisy, pride and lying in plain terms for what they were and so put innocent and simple folk on their guard, and saved them. When the Buddha, with the lamb on his shoulder, went up to the Brahmins who were engaged in an animal sacrifice, it was in no soft language that he spoke to them; he was, however, all love at heart. Who am I in comparison with these? Even so, I aspire to be their equal in love in this very life . . .[7]

Here Gandhi finds the root of humanity in the faith born of truth and love. And this faith overcomes religious intolerance, prevails against racial and sexual prejudices, and defeats political domination.

From the story of the social worker and Barbar Deva the outlaw to the story of Mahatma Gandhi to the story of the people of India, to the story of Martin Luther King and Dietrich Bonhoeffer, even to the stories of Jesus and the Buddha! Is this not the story of humanity? Is this not part of the stories of human beings in search of their roots in faith, hope, and love?

Stories extend our horizons of knowledge. They expand the limits of our faith. They take us to the roots of our being to perceive the depths of our being in love, truth, and hope. Stories are gifts God has given to

---

6. See Green, *Gandhi in India*, 6.
7. Ibid.

humanity to perceive what is true in a world full of dishonesty, to witness what is good in God's creation exposed to evil, and to contemplate what is beautiful in the heart of each one of us tormented by ugly, selfish thoughts.

It is stories such as these, stories of faith and betrayal, of hope and despair, of love and hostility, that should be the primary sources of theology.

7

Stories within a Story

MANY THINGS IN LIFE start with one kind of assumption or another. Assumption is assumption. In logic it is "a statement that is used as the premise of a particular argument but may not be otherwise accepted."[1] Assumption, to use another expression, is hypothesis, but in fact is more than hypothesis. It is a working presupposition that enables us to go about the business of life and work. Some assumptions are so obvious that we take them for granted and pay no more attention to them. That the sun rises in the east and sets in the west is one of the most common assumptions. It is so common that we no longer ask what life and the world would be like if the sun were to rise in the west and set in the east. So far no scientist has shown that the latter could be true and we join with people of all times and all places to carry on our life and work on the assumption that the sun rises in the east and sets in the west. The point we are making here is that we need some assumptions for what we do and think until those assumptions are proved untrue or not applicable. When that happens, these assumptions will have to be replaced by other assumptions that could better serve what we do whether in our daily activities or in our intellectual endeavors.

Does story theology have assumptions? Just as any other thing in life and endeavor, story theology begins with some basic assumptions. What is one of the most fundamental assumptions of theological engagement with stories? It is this: *there is more than one story within a story*. This assumption implies that each story within a story has a meaning that either illuminates the primary meaning of the story or discloses different

1. *Collins English Dictionary*, 92a.

layers of meaning in the story. That is to say, a story has multiple, and not just singular, meanings. Sometimes these multiple meanings in a story can even contradict each other. We will presently demonstrate what has just been said about this fundamental assumption of story theology.

One recalls at this point that this basic assumption of story theology differs from what was held to be almost a sacrosanct principle of interpreting Jesus' parables in the Gospels a few decades ago, namely, each of Jesus' parables has one meaning, and one only.

THE STORY OF ABRAHAM OFFERING ISAAC AS A SACRIFICE

As has been pointed out, that there are many stories within a story is a basic assumption of story theology. Chinese idioms such as "the music hidden in the music played by a stringed instrument," (*shuan wai chi yin*) or "hidden meanings between the lines" (*yan wai chi yi*), are vivid metaphors of this. Is this not the case with philosophical treatises, theological writings, political speeches, social discourses, and daily conversations? This assumption should apply practically to all stories as well.

To illustrate this basic assumption of story theology, let us explore in more than one way the well-known story of Abraham offering Isaac as a sacrifice to God. The story is found in the twenty-second chapter of the book of Genesis in the Hebrew Bible. One cannot but agree that "this story is one of the most brilliantly told narratives"[2] in the book of Genesis. It is a fascinating story, too, as it yields to the questioning mind layer after layer of meanings not obvious to most readers and commentators.

Story 1: God Tested Abraham?

Let us begin with the most obvious, that is, reading the story, as most readers do, as a story of "God testing Abraham." Does not the story open with the statement that "after all these things God tested Abraham" (Gen 22:1)? What does the author of the story have in mind in this statement? Is it not self-evident? Is it not transparent? "The statement in the opening verse," we are told, "that God's purpose in demanding Isaac's death was to test Abraham's obedience—to see whether he 'feared God' (v.12)—is an

---

2. Barton and Muddiman, *Oxford Bible Commentary*, 53b.

accurate summary of the plot."[3] It is also observed that "the drama takes its beginning from God, and finds its resolution in God."[4] Did the story begin with God? This is the question we are going to explore.

It seems apparent that the author had God begin the story. He told it "with great psychological sensitivity and stylistic skill,"[5] but did he want the main plot of his story to be God testing Abraham and nothing else? Was it his purpose to show how Abraham feared God even to the point of offering Isaac his son as a sacrifice to God? Was his chief motive to testify how Abraham, the revered patriarch, passed the test of faith? But does the great "psychological sensitivity and stylistic skill" with which the author told the story only apply to Abraham and not to anyone else inside and outside the story? No attempt has been made in the history of interpretation to deal with other actors in the story with equal "psychological sensitivity and stylistic skill." The stage is supposed to be filled entirely by God and Abraham. It is the drama that took place between God and Abraham. But the questions such as we raised compel us to search for other unfamiliar stories in this familiar story. And these unfamiliar stories we are going to uncover may tell us something quite different about this familiar story.

Story 2: "Take your Son, your only Son . . ."

Abraham took his son Isaac on a journey to the land of Moriah. The storyteller did not tell us how old Isaac was when Abraham took Isaac with him to Moriah. Isaac in the story appeared to be an unsuspecting child enjoying his father's company on a three-day journey. It could be the first time he was going to be away for almost a week. He felt happy and safe in the company of the two young servants and particularly his father's company. The trees and flowers along the mountain roads seemed to smile at him. Birds on the trees greeted him with chirping and singing. The fresh mountain air energized him and the stars at night seemed to be telling him endless stories.

From time to time Abraham looked at his son Isaac and tried to talk to him. But his words stopped in his mouth. How could he talk to his son since he knew the purpose of the journey? Isaac was telling

---

3. Ibid.

4. Westermann, *Genesis 12–36*, 364.

5. Barton and Muddiman, *Oxford Bible Commentary*, 53b.

him how glad he was to take him with him. Isaac's innocence pained Abraham all the more. How could he share in his son's excitement as his little son tried to keep up with his pace? He was entirely absorbed in himself, even felt restless. He felt something like a heavy stone weighing on his mind. He did not ignore Isaac entirely, but he did not dare to look at him straight in the eyes; he had to avert his eyes from his son.

Before they had left home, Abraham did tell his son Isaac that the purpose of the journey was to offer a sacrifice to God. As Isaac saw him cut wood and load it on the donkey, he had asked him if they were offering a sacrifice to God. He had to say yes, but did not elaborate on it. Fortunately, Isaac soon forgot the question and could not wait to make the journey. Looking at the happy and unsuspecting child, Abraham must have shuddered at what he was going to do to him.

Story 3: "Stay here with the Donkey . . ."

Abraham took two of his young men on the journey. They were the family servants charged with the responsibility to look after Isaac and to help with the rituals of sacrifice when they reached the land of Moriah. In the story they were silent, but it was oppressive silence. They too knew the purpose of the journey, but they were puzzled when the most important thing was missing in what they had brought with them: a lamb. They asked Abraham, their master, about it and even suggested to him that they should bring one with them. But Abraham looked at them annoyed. He only said to them what he was to say to his son Isaac just before the sacrifice was to take place: "God himself will provide it" (Gen 22:7).

The two young men were still puzzled and looked at each other confused. But since the master said so, they kept their silence and did not say anything further. But a strange thing happened. When they came near the place where the sacrifice was to take place, Abraham ordered them and said: "Stay here with the donkey; the boy and I will go over there; we will worship, and then will come back to you" (Gen 22:5). This was a strange order. Did they not come all the way to assist in the ritual of sacrifice? Why did their master order them to stay away? And the way he ordered them to stay behind was a little unnerving. His voice was trembling a little, his tone was stern, and his face was a little forbidding. This was not the master they used to know. But since this was what their master ordered, they could only obey.

Then they saw Abraham do something that made them even more puzzled. Abraham "took the wood of burnt offering and laid it on his son Isaac, and he himself carried the fire and the knife" (22:6). They knew what the fire and the knife were for, but laying the wood of sacrifice on Isaac? They could not understand it! That made Isaac, the little boy, look like a sacrificial lamb! A dark thought crossed their minds: Is their master going to offer Isaac, his son, to God as a sacrifice? What an absurd idea! It is ridiculous! They quickly put that thought out of their minds and saw them off, the father with the fire and the knife in his hands and the son bearing on his back the wood of sacrifice. *What a curious sight!* They thought as they watched father and son disappear in the distance.

Story 4: "Father, Where is the Lamb for a Burnt Offering?"

Father and son now proceeded to the spot where the sacrifice was to be made, leaving the two young men behind them. Abraham took the wood from the donkey and "laid it on his son Isaac" (22:6). Isaac knew the purpose of their journey and wondered why his father laid the wood of the burnt offering on his back. But where is the lamb for a burnt offering? Isaac was mystified and then grew a little anxious, not about himself but about the fact that no lamb was in sight. With a lingering question in his mind, he set off with his father on the last leg of their journey. But somehow Isaac could not put the question out of his mind. He could not resist asking his father: "Father! The fire and the wood are here, but where is the lamb for a burnt offering?"(22:7).

Abraham was taken off guard by his son's matter-of-fact question. His face became more tense and nervous. But how could he tell his son what was going to happen to him? How could he reveal to his son the secret he had hidden in his heart? All he could say was: "God himself will provide the lamb for a burnt offering, my son" (22:8). He knew his son was going to be the lamb of the burnt offering. But how could he tell his son about it? Did the thought cross his mind to call off this horrible thing he was going to do to his son? Was he seized by the desire to grab his son's hand, turn round and go home?

Isaac soon stopped worrying about the lamb. Since his father said so, God would provide it for them. He was all excited, for at last he was going to witness the most solemn ritual of his religion, the ritual of offering a lamb to God to show faith and loyalty to God. He tried to share his excitement with his father, but his father was unresponsive. He was deep in thought, his face serious, distorted with pain. But how could his son know what was going through his father's mind?

When father and son reached the place of sacrifice, Isaac looked around, but a lamb was still not in sight. When he looked up at his father, his father did not look his usual self. His father was getting more tense and nervous with every passing moment. His father then went about "building an altar and laid the wood in order" (22:9) without saying a word. It was a tense silence, an unbearable silence. Even Isaac could sense it.

Then before Isaac knew what was happening, Abraham "bound his son Isaac, and laid him on the altar, on top of the wood" (22:9). Isaac was too stunned to say a word at first, then all of a sudden he realized that he was going to be the sacrificial lamb. He was frightened. He yelled and cried in protest, but it was to no avail. He saw his own father "reach out his hand, take the knife to kill him" (22:10). At that moment what Isaac saw was not his father who nurtured him, but a stranger, a murderer about to take his life. Completely helpless, tears streamed down his face. He was terrified.

The next thing he realized, through fear and tears, was that the hand of his father holding the knife stopped in mid-air. His father did not bring down the knife on him and kill him. Did his father have second thoughts about it? Did he dread what he was going to do to his son? How could Isaac know? All he knew was that his father was perhaps going to spare his life. He was still frightened, but the nightmare of horror seemed to be over. There appeared from nowhere a lamb. A poor lamb! Abraham took the lamb and offered it as a burnt offering to God.

Father and son left the place of sacrifice, and started on the return journey, joined by the two servants. It was another long three-day journey, but it was a very different journey. Isaac was not chattering and dancing. He was not paying attention to the trees, flowers and birds on the way. He was quiet, deep in thought, not even looking up at his father. That extraordinary experience in the land of Moriah changed him. His father was now a complete stranger to him, one who attempted to take his life. He still could not understand it. All he knew was that his father, his own father, tried to kill him and offer him as a sacrifice to God.

It was a long, long journey. Father and son, though walking side by side, were miles apart, each thinking different thoughts, each preoccupied with different things: pain, remorse and anguish on the father's part, disappointment, heartbreak, and anger on the part of the son. The incident made Isaac grow up prematurely. It marked the beginning of his growing apart from his father. A different kind of relationship began to form between them. The incident also made Abraham realize that he could not do whatever he wished with his son, that he could not simply impose his own religious conviction on his son.

Story 5: What about Sarah, Mother of Isaac?

The absence of Sarah, Isaac's mother in the story, is conspicuous. Why was she left out completely in the story? Why was she not heard in it? What did she do when father and son returned home from their journey? Since nothing is mentioned about her in the story, one has to reconstruct her response to what had happened to Isaac in Moriah.

For father and son the long journey had finally come to an end. At long last they arrived home. Waiting for them was Sarah, mother of Isaac. Ever since her husband and son had left home to offer a sacrifice to God, she looked forward to their return, especially the return of her beloved son Isaac. When she saw them in the distance, she could not hold herself back any longer. She ran to meet them and to hold her son in her arms.

But immediately she sensed something strange in her son. Then turning her eyes inquisitively to Abraham, her husband, she sensed something unusual in him too. They both were serious and behaved formally to each other. Sarah was at first puzzled, then became aware that something unusual must have happened between father and son. She took Isaac aside to ask him what had happened. At first Isaac refused to speak, only sobbing uncontrollably. After much coaxing, Isaac, like the torrents of water that broke the dam, began telling his mother what had taken place in Moriah. When he described how his father had bound him, placed him on the altar, lifting the knife to kill him and offer him as a sacrifice to God, Sarah could hardly believe what she was hearing. That was absolutely incredulous! That her husband, father of their only son Isaac, born to them in their old age, could attempt to kill their son and offer him as a sacrifice to God is totally insane! But Isaac, her son, was not making up the story.

If the relationship between Abraham and his son became strained after that incident in Moriah, the relationship between him and his wife Sarah became tense too. She realized that a religion could force believers to do something horrible to please their God. She came face to face for the first time with the dark side of religion.

For Sarah, Isaac was her world. He was the meaning and purpose of her life. When Isaac was born, Sarah found at last her own life fulfilled. Overjoyed, she found herself filled with excitement: "God has brought laughter for me; everyone who hears will laugh with me" (Gen 21:6). Why such joy and excitement? The birth of Isaac was for her nothing short of a miracle. Was not Abraham her husband "old, advanced in age, and had ceased to be with her after the manner of women" (18:11)? It was to this Sarah that God promised a son (18:10). God kept the promise and Sarah gave birth to Isaac. No wonder she cared for him as "the apple of her eye."

Abraham knew all this. He knew that to take Isaac' life, even if for the purpose of sacrificing him to God, was to take the life of Sarah, his wife. But for him Isaac remained the only card in his hand to bargain with God to make God's promise to him come true. He must act without telling Sarah. All he had told her was that he planned to take Isaac on a journey to Moriah to offer a sacrifice to God. It never occurred to Sarah that her husband was planning to kill Isaac and offer him as a sacrificial lamb to God. Had she had an inkling of it, she would never have let her son leave with his father. To her great relief, her husband's plan was aborted and she had her son back, although confused and bruised.

Story 6: Abraham Tested God

Poor Abraham! His mind was in turmoil and his heart was on fire. He had mulled over God's promise to him long and hard. He could not put away what he had believed God to be saying to him when he decided to take his family and set out on a long and arduous journey from his home in Mesopotamia to the foreign land of Palestine. He was convinced that God had said to him:

> Go from your country and your kindred and your father's house
> to the land I will show you. I will make you a great nation, so that
> you will be a blessing. I will bless you, and the one who curses
> you I will curse; and in you all the families of the earth shall be
> blessed. (Gen 12:1–3)

Abraham was convinced that he was acting on God's promise, and he tried to convince Sarah of it.

But things did not turn out as he had wished. Life in rugged Palestine was difficult. He faced danger everywhere. He found himself in the midst of unfriendly neighbors. And it was only in his old age that he was able to have a son. What happened to God's promise to him to become a great nation? Mere survival for him and his family was a great problem. How could he then become a blessing to all the families of the earth?

Did God go back on God's words? If God did go back on God's words, I, Abraham, must remind God of those words. *If God had forgotten God's promise to me, I must help God recall it. But how?* By offering to God the most precious thing he had in the world. What was his most precious thing in the world? Isaac, his son, the only son he and his wife Sarah were able to have in their old age. He was horrified by the thought and tried to brush it away, but it kept coming back to him. *If I want God to act on God's promise to me, I too must act to get God to fulfill God's promise!*

It was a gamble of faith for Abraham. He loved Isaac dearly, as dearly as his wife Sarah did, but he had to force God to keep the promise and make him "a great nation" through whom "all the families on the earth shall be blessed." He did not have the heart to tell Sarah, his wife, what he was going to do. How could he? If she got wind of it, she would do everything in her power to prevent it. No, she must not be told. It was between him and God. All he could do was to explain to her afterwards why he had to kill their beloved son Isaac, to offer him to God as a sacrifice, and ask for her understanding and forgiveness.

But as the saying goes, "A human proposes, but God disposes." Fortunately for Abraham his plan was frustrated. It was of course fortunate for Isaac and Sarah as well. At the last minute a lamb was found to replace Isaac and Isaac's life was spared. And the patriarchal story went on without interruption. The promise to Abraham to become a great nation was only realized many centuries later when King David founded a nation that dominated the ancient Near Eastern world, but soon it deteriorated on account of internal corruption and the interference of external powers. The dream of becoming "a blessing to all nations of the earth" never came true.

On his way back home from the land of Moriah Abraham realized that it was not God who was testing him but he who was testing God, that it was not God's hand that was forcing him but his hand that was forcing God. Nor was it God testing his loyalty by demanding that Isaac be offered as a sacrifice but him testing God to see if God would keep God's promise to him. He now remembered that at that critical moment when he was about to do something he would regret for the rest of his life, he heard a voice say to him: "Do not lay your hand on the boy or do anything to him" (22:12). Was it God's voice? Was it the voice of his conscience? He said to himself over and over again on the way home: "I must not test God again."

THE STORY OF JESUS' PASSION

For discussion on "stories within a story," we next choose the story of Jesus' passion. The story is far from simple and straightforward; it was the Apostle Paul who made it a theologically simple and straightforward story when he wrote, for example, in his letter to the Christians at Rome:

> For while we were still weak, at the same time Christ died for the ungodly. . . . But God proved his love for us in that while we were still sinners Christ died for us. Much more surely, then, now that we have been justified by his blood, will we be saved through him from the wrath of God. For if while we were enemies, we were reconciled to God through the death of his Son, much more surely, having been reconciled, we will be saved by his life. (5:6–12)

This is the Apostle Paul's "story of Jesus' death" in a nutshell. It is more of a theology than a story. When one reads this theological statement carefully, one is struck by expressions such as human sin and weakness, God's wrath, and Jesus' death as reconciliation between God and us "enemies" of God.

One recalls Paul's visionary experience of the risen Jesus on his way to Damascus to arrest Jesus' followers. It was a traumatic experience that completely changed him from one who tyrannized Jesus' followers to one who became a tireless propagator of the faith he had done everything in his power to stamp out. It is evident that this personal conversion of his radically affected not only his life but his religious orientation. This "theology of Jesus' death" was very much a theology rooted in his experience of conversion and developed from it. It was this *personal* story of Jesus' death that was to become the *official* theology of redemption for the entire Christian church after him. It was also to become the main version of redemption for most Christians in the next two thousand years. The whole story of Jesus' passion has been viewed from his personal experience of conversion. It has become prescriptive for the church's theology of Jesus' death and most Christians' faith in Christ as the Son of God, the only savior of the whole world.

But there are many other players in the story of Jesus' passion. These other players lived and worked with Jesus for three years. Paul never lived and worked with Jesus. While those others were present at the last supper Jesus had with them before his arrest and crucifixion, Paul was not a part of it. The story of Jesus' passion was anything but simple and straightforward. It was made up of more than one story, each story shedding a different light on it. Without these stories, it is impossible to get at more or less the actual state of affairs surrounding it. We must, therefore, probe the various stories involving some other players. And of course the main player in the passion story is Jesus himself. So we will begin with Jesus, with his final entry into Jerusalem.

Story 1: "If these were silent, the stones would cry out" (Luke 19:40)

It was a tumultuous scene. Jesus rode on a donkey entering Jerusalem, surrounded by the excited crowd. They were shouting at the top of their voices, saying: "Blessed is the king who comes in the name of the lord! Peace in heaven" (Luke 19:38).

Some of the Pharisees in the crowd were worried. They were aware of the Roman soldiers watching them at a distance poised to strike if the procession were to turn into insurrection. They were well-meaning religious leaders eager to prevent the violence of Roman soldiers against Jews. Alarmed and agitated, they approached Jesus and said to him: "Teacher, order your disciples [followers] to stop" (19:39). Jesus understood their concern, but instead of asking his followers to be more discreet, he said to the religious leaders in reply: "I tell you, if these were silent, the stones would cry out" (19:40).

Jesus' reply was "to pour oil on the flame," as it were. The religious leaders were horrified, but the people were delighted. Jesus was not ordering them to stop; instead, he was encouraging them to shout out loud all the more! These stones! These stones in Jerusalem and in their own land have been kept silent for a long time. What are these stones? They are Jews under the oppressive Roman rule. And Jesus was one of the oppressed Jews. Now the time has come for them to shout out loud for all to hear, including the Roman authorities.

Story 2: "Look, the world has gone after him!" (John 12:19)

There were other religious leaders who were not so well-meaning as those who, out of concern and fear, asked Jesus to stop his followers from shouting. Jesus challenged the power and authority they wielded over the helpless people. He disputed their teaching about religious traditions. He questioned their effort to maintain peace with the Roman rulers in order to protect their vested interests. To them he was a thorn in the side. Seeing the crowd shouting and following Jesus into Jerusalem, they gnashed their teeth in anger and said to each other: "Look, the world has gone after him!" (John 12:19).

But a sinister counsel prevailed in the end. Calming his agitated colleagues, Caiaphas, the high priest, gestured to them and said slowly but distinctly: "You know nothing at all! You do not understand that it is better to have one man die for the people than to have the whole nation destroyed" (11:49–50). These words sealed the fate of Jesus. The plot was carefully hatched to have Jesus arrested and handed over to the Roman authorities.

Story 3: Thirty Pieces of Sliver (Matt 26:14–16)

The riddle of thirty pieces of silver! For the Christian church it is not a riddle. The thirty pieces of silver are the undisputable evidence of Judas's betrayal of Jesus, Judas who was one of his disciples, who acted as treasurer for Jesus and the disciples. But who was "Judas called Iscariot" (Luke 22:3)? He was from Judea, as his name Judas would indicate. As to Iscariot, his second name, it could have diverse meanings such as "a man from Kerioth," "a man who was a betrayer," "a man who was a liar." It could also have been derived from "Sicarii," "a group of assassins who used knives," in which case Judas Iscariot "was a member of a group called Zealots who fought against the Romans."[6]

Judas Iscariot as Judas Sicarii, a member of a group called "Zealot," offers an important clue to the story of Jesus' passion. He negotiated with the chief priests "to betray Jesus with thirty pieces of silver" (Matt 26:14–16), equivalent to "one hundred and twenty days' wages." But agreeing to accept "the sum of money so trivial for a treachery so heinous, and the motive [of avarice so] superficial"?[7]

6. See Learning Bible, 1931 (notes on Luke 22:3).

7. See Buttrick, Interpreter's Dictionary of the Bible, 2:1007a.

Judas Iscariot was among the crowd when Jesus entered Jerusalem. He heard Jesus' reply to the Pharisees: "I tell you, if these were silent, the stones would shout out." Mingling with the crowd, he cheered with them at Jesus' words. He believed that the moment that he and some of his fellow Jews were waiting for had arrived. He slipped out of the crowd to have a clandestine meeting with the religious leaders. He knew they were plotting against Jesus. He could beat them at their own game. He would expose their evil plan when the decisive moment of the revolt against the Romans led by Jesus struck. Judas Iscariot and the religious leaders were harboring entirely different thoughts when they concluded their negotiation over thirty pieces of silver—the religious leaders against Jesus and Judas Iscariot against the Romans.

Then came the Passover meal that turned out to be the Last Supper. Jesus, his disciples and other followers were in a friend's home in Jerusalem, sharing the meal. Everyone present, including Jesus, was sober and tense. The atmosphere of the room was filled with foreboding. The silence was almost unbearable. It was Jesus who broke the silence. As the bread and the wine were distributed, they heard Jesus saying: "This is my body which is given for you. This cup is the new covenant in my blood" (Luke 22:19–20). What did Jesus mean with these words? Was he predicting that the revolt against the Romans was going to be, just as the previous revolts, a bloody affair?

When those present at the meal were pondering over these words of Jesus, they heard Jesus turn to Judas Iscariot and say: "Do quickly what you are going to do" (John 13:27). They did not have a clue of what Jesus meant when he addressed Judas Iscariot in this way. But Judas Iscariot seemed to understand it as a signal from Jesus. He, "after receiving the piece of bread [from Jesus], immediately went out" (13:30) to carry out the plans he had negotiated with the chief priests.

But the plan he had made backfired. The revolt did not take place. The religious leaders in reality beat him at his own game. They had Jesus arrested, tried him at the Jewish Council, and handed him over to the Roman authorities who in turn sentenced him to die on the cross. Judas Iscariot watched the turn of events helplessly. There was nothing he could do. "Nothing short of disillusionment over Jesus, from whom he had hoped so much"[8] shattered him. His naivety and stupidity to negotiate a deal with the religious authorities resulted in

8. Ibid.

the tragic death of his master. He felt so remorseful and dejected that he lost the will to live. He took his own life and died a tragic death himself (Matthew 27:3–5; Acts 1:18).

Story 4: "Is it I, Lord?" (Mark 14:19)

We have to retrace our steps back to the scene of the Last Supper. In the course of the Passover meal, all of those present heard Jesus say to the disciples: "One of you will betray me, one of you who is eating with me" (Mark 14:18). They looked at each other in surprise, but they were in fact more "distressed" (14:19) than surprised. They were distressed that Jesus used the word "betray." Like everybody else present, none of the disciples thought of betraying Jesus. Peter was sincere when he declared to Jesus: "Even though I must die with you, I will not betray you" (14:31). These words came from the bottom of his heart. But it was not only Peter who said them; "all of them [the disciples] said the same" (14:31). They would stay with him from beginning to end when he led them in a revolt against the Romans. They would never leave him in the lurch.

The disciples were so distressed at Jesus' words that all of them asked him one after another the question: "Is it I, Lord?" (14:19, RSV) Judas Iscariot also asked, as this exchange had taken place before he left the meal to carry out his plans with the religious authorities. "Is it I, Lord?" This was a painful question. It was the question they asked to pledge once again their loyalty to Jesus and to his cause as they understood it. They understood Jesus' rule of God to mean the restoration of the Davidic kingdom, the recovery of their independence from Roman colonial rule, and the establishment of a religious state free from foreign domination. They would not budge from their national cause, even if they had to pay the price for it with their lives.

When Jesus was arrested contrary to their expectation, they realized that their hope was dashed to the ground. They were disillusioned and also frightened. Now that they had lost their cause for which they were prepared to fight to the end, they had to flee to save their own lives. As to Peter, he was still not quite ready to leave Jesus alone to bear all the consequences. He "followed Jesus at a distance right into the courtyard of the high priest" (14:54) to see if something still could be done for Jesus. There he was spotted by one of the servant girls of the high priest, who identified him as a member of Jesus' circle. Instinctively, he denied it vehemently, but when he remembered what Jesus said about his denying Jesus three times before the cock would crow, "he broke down and wept" (14:72). Like Judas Iscariot he was extremely remorseful and dejected, but unlike Judas he chose to live to become a faithful evangelist who ended his life as a martyr in Rome, the capital city of the Roman Empire that colonized his people.

Story 5: "Have nothing to do with that innocent man" (Matt 27:19)

In spite of the fact that everyone knew Jesus was innocent, that he had not committed any crime, only one dared to intervene for him—the wife of Pontius Pilate, the Roman procurator.

Only the author of Matthew's Gospel tells us the incident. According to his account, "while Pilate was sitting on the judgment seat, his wife sent word to him, 'Have nothing to do with that innocent man, for today I have suffered a great deal because of a dream about him" (27:19). What is one to make of it? Is this a part of "the process which was to grow: the progressive exoneration of Pilate and the placing of full blame on the Jews"?[9] There was a certain truth in this, but the situation was much more complicated than that. What was it, then?

Who was Pilate's wife? Her identity is shrouded in mystery. The only thing we know about her is that she was Pontius Pilate's wife. She might have been a secret admirer of Jesus. She might even have been a clandestine follower of Jesus' way, like the secret Japanese Roman Catholics four hundred years ago when Christianity was prohibited on pain of death by the feudal government.

This could be what her dream is telling us. At least she was not indifferent to Jesus, that strange preacher from Galilee. She neither saw him nor heard him in person, but the message of God's rule he preached and his ministry to the poor and the distressed left a deep impression on her. He moved about in great freedom without fear. He was all compassion to the poor and the oppressed. What a contrast to the naked Roman power and its brutal authority! That man Jesus not only preached about God's love and justice but practiced them. She dreamed about him abused and tortured by his enemies. In her dream she saw him die a tragic death on the cross. It was a nightmare and she woke up in horror. How could that man be guilty of the accusations people were heaping upon him?

9. Ibid., 3:812a.

He must be rescued from his adversaries intent on his death. But how? The only person in the whole world who could still save his life was Pontius Pilate, the Roman procurator sitting in the judgment seat. Her husband alone has the power and authority to spare his life. She must let him know of her bad dream before it was late. That was all she was able to do.

But she overestimated her husband's power. The power he had came from Caesar, the Roman Emperor. And he must use that power to placate his Jewish subjects. The crowd was shouting for Jesus' death and was almost out of his control. He said to Jesus: "Do you not know that I have the power to release you, and the power to crucify you?" (John 19:10) Pilate had the power to release Jesus, but he did not dare to use that power because he was afraid of the shouting crowd in front of his headquarters. He had the power to crucify Jesus and he abused it to have Jesus crucified on the cross. Jesus was right when he answered Pilate: "You would have no power over me unless it had been given you from above . . ." (19:11). Unfortunately, the power Pilate had was not given from above. Jesus knew Pilate was powerless before the Roman Emperor and the excited crowd.

The last intervention to save Jesus by Pilate's wife was futile. Pilate sentenced Jesus to die on the cross, ostentatiously washing his hands in water, declaring he was innocent of Jesus' death (Matt 27:24). This act of his was "hypocritical."[10]But he was to be remembered as the Roman governor in Palestine who became instrumental in Jesus' death. His wife disappeared completely from the pages of history.

Story 6: "Daughter of Jerusalem, do not weep for me"

The road from Pontius Pilate's headquarters to Golgotha outside the city where the crucifixion was to take place is about three hundred yards. It was a short distance, but for Jesus, after cruel tortures by the Roman soldiers and bearing the heavy cross, it was a long distance. He stumbled, fell and was forced to get on his feet again to move towards the place of the crucifixion. As he continued his tortuous trek, he saw and heard among the great number of people following him "women beating their breast and wailing for him" (Luke 23:27) in an uncontrollable bursts of sorrow and lament.

---

10. Barton and Muddiman, *Oxford Bible Commentary*, 881b.

Among these women was Mary his mother. Her nightmare had come true, the nightmare that she wanted to forget since the day when she had brought the eight-day-old Jesus to be blessed by old Simeon at the temple of Jerusalem. She never forgot what he had said to her as they were leaving the temple: "This child is destined for the falling and the rising of many in Israel, and to be a sign that will be opposed so that the inner thoughts of many will be exposed—and a sword will pierce your own soul too" (Luke 2:34–35). It does not matter whether this was actually said by old Simeon more than thirty years back or was a reflection on the part of Luke the author when he was recounting the life of Jesus. For Mary her nightmare came true when she saw her son dragging himself painfully to his certain death. She felt "a sword piecing her own soul."

There was another Mary (John 12:3) among the women. Jesus was invited to have a meal in the house of Simon the leper (Mark 14:3). Knowing that Jesus was in Simon's house,[11] she "came with an alabaster jar of very costly ointment of nard, and broke open the jar and poured the ointment on his head" (14:3) The disciples did not understand the meaning of what she was doing and rebuked her for it. But Jesus saw the meaning of her action and was reported to have said: "She has anointed my body beforehand for its burial. Truly I tell you, wherever the good news is proclaimed in the whole world, what she has done will be told in remembrance of her" (14:8–9). Mary was now with other women beating her breast and wailing for him. Just as her mother, his soul was pierced by a sword too.

But Jesus sensed that there was something much more than his own personal tragedy, something greater than the sorrow of these women. Jesus, in spite of his unbearable pain, addressed them as "daughters of Jerusalem" and said: "Do not weep for me, but weep for yourselves and for your children" (Luke 23:28). Then he added something that may be cryptic to us today but was perhaps obvious to the women he was addressing: "For if they do this when the wood is green, what will happen when it is dry?" (23:31). What was Jesus referring to? The reference "is most likely to the destruction of Jerusalem in 70 CE [carried out by the

---

11. According to Luke's account (Luke 7:36) the meal took place at the house of one of the Pharisee.

Roman forces]. Compared with Jesus, Jerusalem and her people take on the characteristics of a dead tree."[12]

Jesus' personal tragedy foreshadowed the national tragedy. This is why he asked these women lamenting his tragedy to lament the national tragedy to be inflicted on them. His crucifixion portended a national disaster that could not be averted.

Story 7: "Not what I want, but what you want" (Mark 14:36)

The stories surrounding Jesus' crucifixion re-created in the foregoing pages show reasonably clearly that it was brought about by the religious and political authorities combined against him. Jesus was arrested in the garden of Gethsemane, first brought to the Jewish Council for questioning, then turned over to the Roman authorities for his trial and death sentence.

But how did Jesus himself regard the series of events that led to his death? There does not seem to be a conclusive answer to the question. Still it is the most critical question because Jesus is the main actor in the drama after all. It was his trial. It was his death sentence. And it was his death on the cross. It is not possible for us to get into the mind of Jesus to perceive what is happening there. But it is still important to hazard a guess on the basis of scant evidence in the story of his passion in the Gospels. We are thus taken back to the garden of Gethsemane in which Jesus spent his past hours before he was arrested.

In Gethsemane one is given a glimpse of Jesus praying to God. At one point he prays so fervently that "his sweat became like great drops of blood falling down on the ground" (Luke 22:44). His prayer revolves around the central question of what he wants and what God wants of him. "Abba, Father, for you all things are possible; remove this cup from me; yet not what I want, but what you want" (Mark 14:36) This prayer holds a clue to our search for an answer to the question of how Jesus might have striven in his own mind to face his death.

In actual fact, this is not such an extraordinary prayer. Many believers make such a prayer to God when faced with a very difficult decision in life, especially a decision that could affect their career profoundly. And Jesus in Gethsemane is faced with the most momentous decision in his life—to be arrested without resistance, to rise in revolt against

---

12. Barton and Muddiman, *Oxford Bible Commentary*, 957a.

Roman colonial rule, or to disappear somewhere to stage a comeback? It is a life-and-death decision.

What does Jesus really want when he says in his prayer "not what I want"? What does he want if he has his own way? What does he want if he follows his own instinct? What does he want as he and his fellow Jews chafe under the oppressive Roman rule? What doe he want when his own religious authorities are undermining the security of his nation in collaboration with the Roman authorities? What does he want when he looks at the emaciated faces of the children and the poor lives of men and women longing for a better life?

Jesus remembers how the crowd welcomed his entry into Jerusalem only a few days earlier. Did they not shout at the top of their voices acclaiming him as "the one who comes in the name of the lord and the coming kingdom of our ancestor David" (Mark 11:9–10)? And when some religious leader tried to silence them, did he not say: "I tell you, if these were silent, the stones would cry out" (Luke 19:40)? He also remembered what he said to Pontius Pilate towards the end of the trial: "You say that I am a king. For this I was born, and for this I came into the world, to testify to the truth. Everyone who belonges to the truth listens to my voice" (John 18:37). Jesus was not boasting. He did command the hearing of the people who gathered around him. To them he was a king, the one who came in the name of the Lord!

All this Jesus remembered, and all this is what he wanted. But he goes on to pray in Gethsemane: "yet, not what I want, but what you (God) want." What does God want? Is it different from what he wants? Is it opposed to what he wants? Does it contradict what he wants? Questions such as these went through his mind, making him extremely restless. Does God want him to submit to his arrest, trial and death on the cross? What horrible shame, pain and suffering would all this bring to him? It is a bitter cup he prays God to remove from him (Mark 14:36).

But in his agony on the cross Jesus also remembers what he said to Pontius Plate: "My kingdom is not of this world. If my kingdom were from this world, my followers would be fighting to keep me from being handed over to the Jews. But as it is, my kingdom is not from here" (John 18:36). My kingdom is not of this world! Pilate was relieved to hear Jesus say it. But Jesus also declared that if it were not the case "his followers would be fighting for him." Pilate heard these words as a threat.

He found the justification to crucify Jesus to prevent him from leading people in revolt against Rome.

Pilate took these words as political words, but for Jesus these were religious words, words to decide whether to follow what he wanted or to follow what God wanted. After the agonizing time spent with God in Gethsemane, he finally decided that his arrest, trial and death on the cross was what God wanted. He knew the unbearable pain and suffering in what God wanted from him, but in a strange way what God wanted was something entirely different. In a curious way it came from Caiaphas the high priest in his shrewd and at the same time sinister remark made to the other religious leaders as he plotted against Jesus: "You know nothing at all! You do not understand that it is better for you to have one man die for the people than to have the whole nation destroyed" (John 11:49–50).

The death of Jesus on the cross did prevent the whole nation from being destroyed, but it did not avert the catastrophe of 70 CE when Jerusalem fell to the onslaught of the Roman legions. Perhaps it is in light of the destruction of the nation that the second half of Jesus' prayer in Gethsemane, "but what you [God] want," takes on the theological meaning of the crucifixion that has dominated the faith of the Christian church and most Christians. And it is the Apostle Paul, as we mentioned at the outset of this chapter, who laid the foundation of the theology of the cross with its focus on salvation of the soul as the sole meaning of Jesus' life and death at the expense of many a story of men and women surrounding Jesus' passion story.

8

Stories Are Culturally Distinctive

MANY STORIES WITHIN A story! In the previous chapter we selected two stories, one from the Hebrew Bible, the other from the New Testament, to show how they are made up of many stories that directly or indirectly divulge the meanings only implicit in them. This, to use a Chinese idiom, is to look for "something more in what is said," literally "there are paintings in a painting" (*huah chong yeou huah* in Chinese).

At first this sounds like an aberration from the ways in which most of us are schooled to interpret the Bible, but on second thought we are prompted to ask: Is this not how we may get at the meanings not only explicit but more importantly implicit in a passage or story in the Bible? As a matter of fact, is this not what most people do, scholars and lay believers alike, when engaged in efforts to understand what the author of a passage or story in the Bible meant?

The question for us is how to "elicit meanings between the lines, hear the sound outside the sounds produced by musical instruments, or let the hidden meanings between the lines speak out." The question challenges Western biblical scholars and theologians who have monopolized the interpretation of the Bible. It throws wide open the door of interpretation to men and women from outside the West, to people of different ethnic origins and cultural backgrounds, to women as well men, to the powerless over against those who hold power, whether political, social, religious, or academic.

We have now arrived at the threshold of an exciting new world of interpretation. How do we then enter this exciting new world? How do we go about engaging ourselves in efforts to see the images, hear the sounds and penetrate the world of love, faith, pain, suffering and hope, hidden in the depths of human hearts? In this chapter and the next we will focus our efforts on finding our ways in this new world of understanding and interpreting stories in the Bible and in different cultural-religious settings. We will explore how stories are culturally distinct one from the other and yet how they can be theologically interactive. In other words, we need to develop methods through which the familiar stories in the Bible and stories from outside the Bible will tell us meanings unfamiliar to us, disclose to us the world so far hidden from us, and reveal to us the inner world of women and men whose internal world is similar to ours in more ways than one.

STORIES ARE CULTURALLY DISTINCTIVE

Stories play a key role in our story theology. This seems a matter-of-fact statement, but it is anything but matter-of-fact. It at once elevates stories to the center stage of the dramas of life and faith in which we are all engaged. And as we already know, the theology worthy of its name has to be part and parcel of the dramas of life and faith.

Story comes in a variety of forms and has different designs. It is a genus, or a type, consisting of a number of species, as it were. It may be called "genres," to borrow a common expression in literature. Story comes in different genres such as fairy tale or household tale, folktale, novella (short prose narrative), animal tale, legend or saga, etiological tale, myth, parable, or story of life and faith. We owe the hard-working folklorists who travel all over the world collecting stories and classifying them into different genres or types.

One of the things that impresses folklorists most is how culture has shaped stories of different genres, in other words, how stories are culturally distinctive. An observation from an extensive study of stories from Japan underlines this point. "*Densetsu* [legend]," it is pointed out, "belong to the living folk-culture of Japan, and are supported by the institutions of the culture, like Shinto shrines and national festivals and Kabuki and Noh drama, which honor the old traditions."[1]

---

1. The observation is made by Richard M. Dorson, an American folklorist; see his *Folk Legends of Japan*, 25.

The Kannon Who Substituted

As an example of how culture not only plays an essential and intrinsic part in stories but gives stories distinctive characteristics, we invite you to listen to this Japanese story called "The Kannon Who Substituted." This is how the story goes:

> Looking up from a small village nestled at the foot of a certain mountain, one can see a little shrine of Kannon on the very top. A young couple used to live in that village. The wife, for all her youth, believed in Kannon with utmost sincerity. Every night, after she had finished her daily housework she visited the shrine to worship the image. Her husband did not know the reason for her going and became suspicious of the wife who went out and returned to the house every night at the same time. One day he finally lost patience and determined to kill her. So he hid in the dark woods by the roadside and waited for his wife to come back. At the usual time she returned. The husband watched her coming near and carefully aiming at her shoulder, swung down his sword askance. At this moment the wife felt her blood run cold throughout her body.
>
> The husband wiped the blood from his sword and put it back in its sheath. When he returned to his home, he was astonished to see his wife, whom he thought he had slashed to death. He marveled, and went back to see the place where he had struck his wife. Sure enough, there were the dots of blood on the ground. He retraced his steps homeward, and asked his wife: "Didn't you feel something strange at such and such a time in such and such a place?" Then the wife answered: "Just at that time something made my blood run cold." The husband could not but confess all that had happened.
>
> The next morning he wakened early and was surprised to see the blood dotted all the way from the entrance of his house to the shrine on top of the mountain. When he looked at the statue of Kannon, he was again surprised to see a scar on the statue's shoulder, on the place where he had struck his wife the night before.
>
> Now this Kannon is still popular in the neighboring villages, and they celebrate a festival for her on January 24 every year.[2]

This is an exquisitely told *legend*, "a story handed down for generations among a people and popularly believed to have a historical basis,

---

2. See Dorson, *Folk Legends of Japan*, 39–40.

although not verifiable."[3] It is deeply rooted in the Japanese Buddhist culture of Kannon, the goddess of mercy.

This story-legend is almost like a Japanese painting, enabling you not only to hear it, but to see the isolated village surrounded by the mountains atop one of which is the shrine of Kannon, the focus of the villagers' religious devotion. Against this background of serene nature and religious devotion is the mercy of Kannon, the goddess of mercy, who shielded the young wife from her husband's deadly blow.

Everything in this legend is distinctively Buddhist, not the elitist kind of Buddhism taught at prestigious temples or Buddhist universities but popular Buddhism demonstrated in the faith of farmers, laborers, and small shop keepers in remote villages and rural areas. Set in this popular Buddhist culture, the legend speaks out of the spirits and souls of indigenous Japanese men and women born to live and die not knowing the wide world existing beyond the seas surrounding their nation.

This is distinctively a Buddhist story. Reset in a different religious culture, the legend would change its color, shape and nuance. There would be no Kannon statue on top of a mountain in an isolated Japanese village. There would be no Japanese samurai husband who only knew how to let his sword speak against his wife to vindicate his honor. There would be no obedient Japanese wife accepting death rather than defending herself as Japanese custom and tradition demanded. And there would be no Kannon statue that saved the wife from harm's way with the blood of Kannon, the goddess of mercy.

The legend is in every way Japanese from beginning to end, from inside out. And yet, it moves those from other religious backgrounds and interacts with stories from other religious cultures. Why? We will try to answer this question in the second half of this chapter. At present we must continue to listen to some other stories from another culture.

The Keys of Destiny

From Japan we now travel to Persia. Speaking of Persia, what comes to mind at once is *Arabian Nights,* also called *The Thousand and One Nights.* It is a collection of Arabic stories. The collection consists of about two hunderd stories that include widely known stories such as Aladdin

---

3. *Webster's New World Dictionary,* 771b.

and the Wonderful Lamp, Ali Baba and the Forty Thieves, and Sinbad the Sailor.

How did these stories come about? The first story, "The Tale of King Shahryar and His Brother," tells us how these stories come to be told. The storyteller is Shahrazad, a beautiful daughter of one of the King's officials. As the legend has it, "King Shahryar has learned that his wife has been unfaithful. He orders her killed and vows to marry a new maiden each night and have her beheaded the next morning." Shahrazad, the beautiful maiden, volunteers to come to the king's bedroom to tell the king a story. The story she tells is "so entertaining that the king allows her to live another day to finish it. One story leads to another, and Shahrazad continues to relate tales for a thousand and one nights. By then, the king has fallen in love with her."[4]

These stories of *Arabian Nights*, if romantic and happy in the end, are hatched in human tragedies. Shahrazad, the beautiful storyteller, has to risk her life to soften the king's heart with one story after another. By telling these stories, though entertaining and sometimes hilarious, she is racing against time and putting her life on the line. Anxiety, fear and death grip her. But tragedy can be the power of human creativity. Exposed to it herself, her storytelling creativity is at work to its fullest, bringing happiness to her and leaving behind her the most famous piece of Arabic literature in the world.

One of the stories, not only entertaining and intriguing but also provocative and inspirational, is called "The Keys of Destiny." It is a long story taking her seven nights to tell. The story begins with "the Khalifah Muhammad ibn Thailun, Sultan of Egypt, as wise and good a ruler as his father had been cruel and oppressive, using his whole power to bring back tranquility and justice to his people." The story is unfolded to him by an old man called Hasan Abdallah who endured forty years of torture and imprisonment at the hands of the Sultan's cruel father because he refused to divulge the secret of alchemy. It turns out to be his own life story.

As Sharhrazad tells the king, Hasan Abdallah was born to a very rich family in Cairo and his father saw to it that he received a good education and married a beautiful wife. He raised his family and lived a happy life for ten years.

---

4. See *World Book Encyclopedia*, 545a.

But who may fathom the intent of Destiny? After those ten years had flowed by like a dream, Fate cast all woes at once upon my house. In a few days my father perished of the plague, fire devoured the buildings of my inheritance, and the waters of the sea swallowed the ships which trafficked into far countries for my gain. I was left as poor as a child robbed of its mother's breast, with no resort save a belief in Allah. . . . My own misery was much, but I grieved more for the destitution of my mother and my wife and my little children . . .

In desperation he accompanied a Badawi, a wealthy man, in exchange for a sum of money to sustain his family, on a long and dangerous journey through the desert to the city of Many-Columned Iran, a Paradise. There the Badawi hoped to find a box "full of red powder" that contained the secret of alchemy. A single grain of the powder could "transmute the vilest metal into gold." With the riches gained from the red powder in the box, the Badawi wanted to "build a mightier palace and raise a more magnificent city than those in the city of Many-Columned Iran, buy the lives of men and the conscience of the pure, seduce virtue herself and make himself a king's son." To Hasan Abdallah's question: "Could you add a day to your life with the powder? or efface a single hour of the past?" the Badawi simply answered: "Allah alone is great!"

While still in the desert on their way to the city of Many-Columned Iran, they

came to a mighty plain which seemed to be made of grains of silver. In the middle of this plain there rose a high column of granite, bearing on its top the upright figure of a youth molded in copper, whose right hand, open and extended, held a heavy key dangling from each of its five fingers. The first key was of gold, the second of silver, the third of Chinese copper, the fourth of iron, the fifth of lead; and all were magical. The man who mastered each had to bear the fate of each, for they were the keys of Destiny: the gold was the key of misery, the silver the key of suffering, the Chinese copper was the key of death, the iron the key of glory, and the lead the key of happiness and wisdom.

The Badawi ordered Hasan Abdallah, being an excellent archer, to shoot down the keys. Knowing the secret of the keys and being a cunning man, the Badawi let Hasan Abdallah keep the gold and silver keys, while he kept the keys of iron and lead. Hasan Abdallah kept the keys of gold and silver in his belt, "not knowing the nature of the keys, and from my ignorance sprang all the misfortunes of my life," including spending many miserable years languishing in prison. Forty years later as he was telling his whole story to the good Sultan, he added pensively: "Yet good and evil come from Allah, and His creature must accept them with humility."

As Hasan Abdallah was about to shoot at "the last key, the key of Chinese copper, not knowing it was the key of death," the Badawi stopped him in the nick of time. They pushed onwards and finally reached the city of Many-Columned Iran. The Badawi found what he wanted—a box of red powder that would turn the vilest metal to gold. They then set out on a journey home. Hasan Abdallah's story continues:

> My first care when I came to Cairo was to run to my own house; but I found none to receive me, neither mother, wife, nor children; the door was broken and open, and wandering dogs had made their home within. Hearing my cries of despair, a neighbor opened his door, saying: "O Hasan Abdallah, may your span be lengthened by the days which these have lost! All your household is dead." . . . I fought down my sobs, and at last gave full rein to my indignation, cursing my companion and accusing him of all my sorrows. He listened in silence and then touched me on the shoulder, saying kindly: "We come from Allah and to Allah we return at last!". . .

After his return to Cairo the Badawi's lot seemed quite different. He built for himself a magnificent palace with the box of the red powder that could turn the basest metal into gold and lived "in the breast of pleasure, and his nights were an anticipation of Paradise." But the red powder that had the alchemistical power was powerless to keep death at bay, or to turn death into life. He died in the midst of luxury and extravagance.

After his companion's death, Hasan Abdallah sought to turn his ignorance to wisdom and his misery to happiness. His heartbreaking story continues:

> I swore to be rid of the fatal keys for ever; so I snatched them from my belt and set them in a crucible upon the fire, until they should be resolved and melt away. While the vessel was heating, I searched everywhere for the other keys, of wisdom and of happiness; but I could find them nowhere. I therefore returned to my crucible and stood watching the fusion of the silver and gold. While I watched, as I thought, my evil luck melting away before my eyes, the pavilion was suddenly invaded by the Khalifah's guards, who bound me and carried me into the presence of their master (the Sultan's cruel father).

Thus began his forty years of imprisonment until he was rescued by the good Sultan to recount to him all the sufferings he had gone through. He "lived honored and respected to the age of one hundred and twenty years, which had been marked for him by Destiny. But Allah knows all! He alone lives, for He dies not!"[5]

This at once fascinating and compelling story belongs to what is called *novella*, "a short narrative tale, a short novel, or novelette, especially a popular story having a moral or satirical [or religious] point."[6] It is set in the religious culture of Islam. The names of the characters in the story are all Arabic names. The God who holds the secret of human destiny is Allah. The story does not move in a straight line; it zigzags, it twists and turns. It begins in Cairo and ends in Cairo, as if things have to return to where they begin. But between the beginning and the end many things have changed, the biggest change being that of human destiny. Nothing remains the same.

The story reminds us of the story of Job in the Hebrew Bible. The central theme in this Arabic story, as in the Jewish story of Job, is the power of destiny against which human beings are helpless and powerless. It is the destiny of Hasan Abdallah to suffer, even though he has not the slightest idea that the keys of gold and silver the Badawi lets him keep are going to make him heartbroken and bring him suffering.

The power of destiny is so strong that even the cunning Badawi could not escape it when death overtakes him in the end, even with all the wealth and prosperity he had acquired with the help of the box of red powder. One cannot help recalling these words of Jesus: "For what will it profit people to gain the whole world and forfeit their life?" (Mark 8:36). As to Hasan Abdallah, he was freed from prison after forty years and "lived honored and respected to the age of one hundred and twenty years, which has been marked for him by Destiny." Destiny does not work on humanity only in negative ways; it also makes human beings taste the joy of heaven in spite of tribulations on earth. The power of destiny can be a healing and redeeming power. In humility and gratitude Hasan Abdallah had to confess, "Allah knows all! He alone lives, for He dies not!" What a faith in Allah!

5. Abridged from Mardrus and Mathers, *Book of the Thousand Nights and One Night*, 488–510.

6. *Collins English Dictionary*, 1069b.

THE UGLY DUCKLING

Even if human destiny is in the hand of Allah, we human beings are not left entirely helpless and totally passive, accepting destiny as irreversible fate. This is the point of "The Ugly Duckling," told by Hans Christian Anderson (1805–1875), a Danish writer.

Han Christian Anderson is a household name to lovers of fairy tales. He wrote 168 fairy tales "based on folklore and observation of people and events in his life. . . . often carrying a moral message for adults as well as children."[7] To this we must add that his fairy tales often carry a "religious" message also.

"The Ugly Duckling," one of Hans Christian Anderson's best-known fairy tales, shortened and condensed here, goes like this. It was a lovely summer in the country, and there was a duck sitting on her nest, hatching out her little ducklings. "At last the eggs cracked open one after the other—'peep! peep!'—and all the yolks had come to life and were sticking out their heads." But the largest egg would not crack.

> "Let's have a look at the egg which won't crack," said the old duck (who had come to pay a call). "I'll bet it's a turkey's egg. . . ." At last the big egg cracked. There was a "peep! peep!" from the young one as he tumbled out, looking so large and ugly. The duck glanced at him and said: "My! What a huge great duckling that is! None of the others look a bit like that. Still, it's never a turkey-chick. . . . Well, we shall soon find out. He shall go into the water, if I have to kick him in myself."

For the big "duckling" it was the beginning of a life of frustration and heartache. He was despised and ostracized by the other ducklings. They vented all their contempt for him when they said:

> "There! Now we've got to have that rabble as well—as if there weren't enough of us already! Ugh! What a sight that duckling is! We can't possibly put up with him"—and one duck immediately flew at him and bit him in the neck. "Leave him alone," said the mother. "He is doing no one any harm." "Yes, but he is so gawky and peculiar," said the one that pecked him, "so he'll have to be squashed." . . .
>
> "What pretty children you have, my dear!" said the old duck with the rag on her leg. "All of them but one, who does not seem right. I only wish you could make him all over again."

---

7. See *New American Desk Encyclopedia*, 58b.

"No question of that, my lady," said the duckling's mother. "He's no pretty, but he is so good-tempered and he can swim just as well as the others—I daresay even a bit better. I fancy his look will improve as he grows up, or maybe in time he'll grow down a little. He lay too long in the egg—that's why he isn't quite the right shape." And then she plucked his neck for him and smoothed out his feathers. "Anyhow, he is a drake, and so it doesn't matter so much," she added "I feel he'll turn out pretty strong and be able to manage all right."

The mother-duck was affectionate to him, lavishing on him her motherly love as she did on her other ducklings. But in a most important respect, she was wrong. She was not able to see something other than a duck in this ugly-looking duckling of hers, believing that he would turn out as pretty a duck when he grew up.

The plight of the ugly duckling worsened. He "got pecked and jostled and teased by ducks and hens alike." He "got shivered about by all of them; even his own brothers and sisters treated him badly . . . The ducks nipped him, the hens pecked him, and the maid who had to feed the poultry let fly at him with her foot." In the end he "didn't know where to turn, was so terribly upset over being so ugly and the laughing-stock of the whole barnyard" that he could not bear it any longer and ran away. Thus began his long, lonely, rough, and bumpy journey towards the discovery of who he really was.

One evening, when there was a lovely sunset, a whole flock of large handsome birds appeared out of the bushes. The duckling had never seen such beautiful birds, all glittering white with long graceful necks. They were swans. They gave the most extraordinary cry, spread out their magnificent long wings and flew from this cold country away to warmer and open lakes. . . . "I will fly across to them, those royal birds!" (the duckling said to himself.) "They will peck me to death for daring, ugly as I am, to go near them. Never mind! Better to be killed by them than be nipped by the ducks, pecked by the hens, kicked by the girl who minds the poultry and suffer hardship in winter." And he flew on to the water and swam towards the beautiful swans. As they caught sight of him, they darted with ruffled feathers to meet him.

The duckling was frightened and felt desperate. He thought this was the end of him.

"Yes, kill me, kill me!" cried the poor creature and bowed his head to the water awaiting his death. But what did he see there in the clear stream? It was a reflection of himself that he saw in front of him, but no longer a clumsy grayish bird, ugly and un-attractive—no, he was himself a swan! . . . Some little children came into the garden and threw bread and grain into the water, and the smallest one called out: "There's a new swan!" and the other children joined in with shouts of delight: "Yes, there's a new swan!" And they clapped their hands and danced about and ran to fetch father and mother. Bits of bread and cake were thrown into the water, and everyone said: "The new one is the pretti-est—so young and handsome!" And the old swans bowed before him . . .[8]

From an ugly duckling to a beautiful swan! What a transformation! If it happened to the ugly duckling, it could happen to every child too! We could almost hear Hans Christian Anderson saying this to a child crying her eyes red and her heart out for love from people around her.

What we have in "The Ugly Duckling" is a fairy tale with the moral and religious theme of transformation. As we have seen, fairy tale is an-other genre of stories. What is then a fairy tale? A fairy tale is commonly understood to be "a story about fairies or other mythical or magical be-ings, especially one of traditional origin told to children."[9] A fairy tale is even said to be highly improbable,[10] unbelievable or untrue.[11]

This characterization of a fairy tale is not entirely correct; it can be even misleading. One recalls the fairy tale of Cinderella, one of the fairy tales collected by the brothers Grimm back in the late eighteenth century and early nineteenth century. In the Disney cartoon version, besides the poor Cinderella later to marry a prince and live happily ever after, the step-mother and the step-sisters who ill treated her, there is a fairy god-mother who, with a wave of her magic wand, changed a pumpkin into a golden chariot drawn by the mice transformed into the flying stallions, carrying her to the ball hosted by the prince to select his princess. The fairy godmother, the golden chariot, and the flying stallions are not real, of course, but is the fairy tale itself is not real? Surely not. The message it conveys is not only probable but true. It inspires a good-hearted person

8. Abridged from Keigwin, *Hans Christian Anderson*, 107–15.

9. See *Collins English Dictionary*, 555b.

10. Ibid.

11. *Webster's New World Dictionary*, 487b.

not to lose heart but to persevere in the face of the mean world of self-interest and malice.

Evidently, we have to go beyond the stereotyped definition of fairy tale if we are to get at the moral and religious meaning embedded in its depths. By *fairy tale* we refer to a story of women, men and children, who struggle to overcome the adversities of the world and to actualize the meaning and purpose of life without compromising their noble heart and honorable conscience. It is crafted from unreal as well as real things, imagined as well as factual beings, to envision a world of moral and religious meanings in contrast to the senseless and inane world.

Let us return to "The Ugly Duckling." Moral and religious transformation is its theme. The theme is moral in that it inspires children and adults alike to realize that life, with all its setbacks, can be transformed from despair to hope, from self-pity to self-respect, and from woe to joy. Its theme is also religious in that what drives people to a religious faith is transformation from sin to forgiveness, from hate to love, and above all, from death to life. Whether moral or religious, "the Ugly Duckling" underlines the point that transformation is internal, that is, something that could happen in one's inner self. It has to be an internal transformation first before it can help bring about the transformation of the outside world.

Transformation is a universal theme to be found in ancient times and today, in the East and in the West. What is then particular about "The Ugly Duckling" and the other fairy tales from Hans Christian Anderson? Is it because he is a Dane and not a Filipino or a Ghanaian? There is a lot to be said for this. As has been pointed out, his "language is full of colloquialisms, special Dutch idioms, untranslatable puns and an intimacy between writer and reader which is strengthened by the frequent use of certain Danish adverbs that defy translation."[12] Unfortunately, the peculiarities of the Danish language are only implicit in the English translation. Perhaps a similar thing can be said of almost all other translations, no matter what languages the translator is dealing with.

The translator of Hans Christian Anderson's fairy tales certainly knows what he is talking about when he says that Hans Christian Anderson

---

12. These are the words of Bredsdorff in his "Introduction" to Keigwin, *Hans Christian Anderson.*

sprinkled his narrative with every kind of conversational touch—crisp, lively openings, to catch the listener's attention at a swoop; frequent asides or parentheses; little bits of Copenhagen slang; much grammatical license; and above all a free use of particles—those nods and nudges of speech. So completely did Anderson maintain the conversational tone in his *Tales* that you are quite shocked when you occasionally come across some really literally turn.[13]

One has to be a native of Denmark or at least have a good command of Danish fully appreciate Anderson's words.

Although what is said here is not always obvious to the reader who is not Danish-speaking and has to rely on the translation, the comment is most germane to the cultural distinctiveness of Hans Christian Anderson's fairy tales. "The Little Mermaid," a fairy tale inspired by the bronze sculpture of the beautiful mermaid sitting on the Danish harbor overlooking the North Sea, is the enchanting story of the mermaid who secretly loved a handsome young prince who thought "she had thrown herself into the waves." But there she was, sitting demurely and pensively on the harbor, shaping for herself an immortal soul by three hundred years of good deeds.[14]

And there is the celebrated tale of "The Emperor's New Clothes," hilariously humorous and bitterly satirical. The vain king succumbed to the two swindlers' scheme and appeared stark naked at grand ceremonies before the stunned eyes of his subjects. Everyone serving the whims of the Emperor all gasped with wonder and said: "Goodness! The Emperor's new clothes are the finest he has ever had. What a wonderful train! What a perfect fit!" But it was a little child who shattered their pretense. In its innocence the child exclaimed: "But the Emperor hasn't got anything on!" That did it and the ice was broken. "'Well, but the Emperor hasn't got anything on!' the people all shouted at last." The pretension crumbled, but not to be defeated, the emperor "drew himself up still more proudly, while his chamberlain walked after him carrying the train that wasn't there."[15] Humorous and satirical too! This is typical of Hans Christian Anderson.

13. These words are from Keigwin, quoted in the "Introduction" to Keigwin, *Hans Christian Anderson*.

14. Hans Christian Anderson, "The Little Mermaid," in Keigwin, *Hans Christian Anderson*, 46–63.

15. Hans Christian Anderson, "The Emperor's New Clothes," in Keigwin, *Hans Christian Anderson*, 64–68.

The setting of "The Ugly Ducking" is as beautiful as the ugly circumstances that surround the duckling before turning into a wonderful swan. So the tale begins: "Summertime! How lovely it was out in the country, with the wheat standing yellow, the oats green, and the hay all stacked down in the grassy meadows! . . . The fields and meadows had large woods all around, and in the middle of the woods there were deep lakes." With this "crisp, lively opening, to catch the listener's attention at a swoop," a most extraordinary transformation is to unfold in the peaceful and serene countryside of Denmark.

Whether it is "The Little Mermaid," "The Emperor's New Clothes," or "The Ugly Duckling," the listener is led to that small nation in Scandinavia called Denmark, to its people, to its history, and to its nature. Stories, be they legend, novella, or fairy tale, are culturally distinctive, displaying the cultural and religious characteristics of the people and the world in which the stories are told and retold. But the strange thing is that these culturally distinctive stories can also be religiously or theologically interactive. It is this dimension, deeply rooted in humanity, that religious teachers and theologians have either overlooked or rejected to their great loss. We must now continue to explore how culturally distinctive stories can be theologically interactive in the following chapter.

9

Stories Can Be Theologically Interactive

IN THE PREVIOUS CHAPTER we dealt with some examples of how stories are culturally distinctive, bearing distinctive characteristics in the cultural settings in which they are told and transmitted. But this does not mean that they are religiously or theologically isolated, having nothing to do with one another. In reality they have a lot to do with one another religiously and theologically. Why can culturally distinctive stories interact with one another religiously and theologically? This is an important question for story theology. It is to this question that we will now turn.

Most stories, no matter to which genre they belong, are addressed to people's social and political concerns. They also grow out of their cultural landscapes. People's social and political concerns, however, are often related to their religious beliefs. This is particularly evident in the ancient world in which theocracy was practiced. Even today there are still a few theocratic states in which social and political concerns are dictated by religious beliefs and laws. In the case of culture, religious concerns are even more evident. After all, culture and religion are twin brothers or sisters, as it were, inseparable at the time of conception and in the embryonic period. The term "religious culture" is used to express the close relationship between religion and culture.

In the course of development, however, culture and religion begin to acquire distinctive features, with culture becoming more and more integrated into the custom and practice of people's daily life, and religion commanding more and more of people's devotion by developing prayers, liturgies, teachings and doctrines, even taboos. Even when cul-

ture becomes secularized, it has not, in reality, parted company with religion. At critical moments in the life of the individual or nation, religion
assumes a prominent role in culture again. For the nation it is the time of
national crisis. A typical example is that of the prophet Isaiah in ancient
Judah in the eighth century BCE. Isaiah himself gives a very dramatic
account of it when he says:

> In the year that King Uzziah died, I saw the Lord sitting on a
> throne, high and lofty; and the hem of his robe filled the temple.
> Seraphs were in attendance above him. . . . And one called to an-
> other, and said:
>
> "Holy, holy, holy is the Lord of hosts,
> the whole earth is full of his glory."
>
> The pivots on the thresholds shook at the voices of those who
> called, and the house filled with smoke. (Isa 6:1–4)

In the year that King Uzziah died. This is what prompted Isaiah to as-
sume his prophetic role. The death of Uzziah, the king of Judah, was a
harbinger of an imminent national crisis, and Isaiah knew it. Before he
could take political action to confront it, he had to repair to the temple
to seek God's will and guidance.

For us individuals, the crises of life often throw us back to our religious sources and resources to face them and seek strength to overcome
them. We recall the famous story of how the Buddha as a young prince
encountered the realities of life—illness, old age and death—in the city.
Shocked and moved, the prince, so the story goes,

> looked back at the city and uttered a lion's roar: "I will not enter
> the city of Kapila until I have seen the other shore of birth and
> death."[1]

He gave up his princely life of luxury and pleasure, went to the forests
to seek emancipation from the life of suffering brought about by birth,
sickness, old age and death.

Whether it is a national crisis or the crises of life for individual
persons such as sickness, old age and death, human beings seek in religion the assurance of life and meaning of it. It is not strange that many
stories of different genres either implicitly or explicitly deal with these
fundamental issues of life common to all humanity. As we have seen, the

---

1. de Barry, *Buddhist Tradition*, 67.

Japanese legend of "The Blood of Kannon" highlights the saving power of the compassion of Kannon, the goddess of mercy, the novella called "The Keys of Destiny" in *Arabian Nights* stresses the power of Allah that transcends pre-determined human destiny, and Hans Christian Anderson's fairy tale, "The Ugly Duckling," maintains that transformation of life is entirely possible.

These are all fundamental religious themes. Because many stories are motivated by them, theological interaction among culturally distinctive stories around these themes is not only possible but vital. Are not most religions at their best, including Christianity, ways to help men and women exposed to adversities of life to find lasting peace and rest in the saving love of God that never fails them? We, Christian or not, should be encouraged to explore how people's stories, stories in the Christian Bible included, theologically interact with one another. Such theological interactions should enable Christians to see the immense diversity and all-embracing power of God's creation on the one hand and, on the other, to grasp the deeper message and significance of God's saving love active in human communities as well as in the Christian community.

Themes or subject matter explored by real-life stories, parables, fables, and myths are many. In what follows we will focus on three of them: *suffering and faith, sin and death, transformation of life*. Our exploration is of a religious and theological nature, since they have preoccupied religions for ages. This means that that folktales revolving around them are not idle tales for entertainment only. They are religious and even "theological" stories equally important as, if not more important than, the official teachings of the religious authorities. They embody people's theology, theology not built on abstract concepts but grown out of people's daily, lived experiences of pain and joy, suffering and hope.

SUFFERING AND FAITH

Our exploration begins with a real-life story called *Alicia's Story* and how it interacts with the story of the woman with hemorrhages in the New Testament (Mark 5:24–34).[2] *Real-life story* should be the primary source of all genres of stories, be they legend, novella, fairy tale, folktale, parable, even myth. It is the most pristine and thus primary source to which other kinds or genres of stories could be traced back. A real-life

2. Also Matt 9:20–22 and Luke 8:43–48.

story is a contemporary story. It is contemporary in a double sense. It is contemporary to the men and women going through the experience in the past. It is also contemporary to the men and women today who go through a similar experience. In the course of time, a real story changes its form or genre and become a legend, a novella, a fairy tale, a folktale, a parable, a myth. But whatever form or genre it may take, it is a *real* life story both to the storyteller and the listener. A story theology that seeks theological interactions with culturally distinctive stories is thus dealing with real stories, and not fictions, whether they come from the past or from the present, no matter in what genre they are told. Is this not why religious scriptures such as the Bible for Christians contain story after story that is old yet forever new, concerning us today as well as others in the remote past?

Alicia's Story

For the theme of suffering and faith we refer to *Alicia's Story*, a real-life story told in first person by a young woman who lives and works in San Francisco, California, and who finds in faith the strength to sustain her through the suffering and pain inflicted on her by cancer. We will at the same time explore how "Alicia's story" today interacts with the story of the woman with hemorrhages in the New Testament in a completely different setting two thousand years ago. We do not know the latter's name, but we know a lot about the suffering and pain she went through. As we have each interact with the other, we will see how these two stories illumine each other to bare the depths of suffering and faith in their hearts and souls and to enable us to perceive the compassionate love of God at work in them.

On March 2, 2000, Alicia Parlette, a twenty-three-year-old *San Francisco Chronicle* copy editor, got a phone call in her office from Dr. Feldman, her doctor. He told her: "Listen, we just got your pathology report back from Stanford from your breast biopsy. They're calling it alveolar soft part sarcoma." Alicia goes on to tell us:

> I froze. I had no idea what that meant. I didn't even know how to spell it. Things you can't begin to spell are never good. Dr. Feldman was still talking. . . . "Wait, wait, hold on. I am not any kind of medical person, so you are going to explain. We're talking about cancer, right? Sarcoma is a kind of cancer?" "Yes, that's right." I was going to throw up. I started wriggling in my chair.

... He told me that I needed a PET scan to determine whether it had spread and that I could probably get one on Friday. Then I'd need another CT scan of my lungs.[3]

With this dreadful news from her doctor, her desperate fight against cancer began. "I hung up the phone," she recalls,

and sat at my desk. I felt the whole weight of his words being shoved down my throat, and I felt my mouth thicken. I stared at my screen for a few minutes. . . . tried to read the story on my computer, but the words didn't make sense. Oh, God, now I couldn't read.

This was followed by a series of PET and CT scans and other tests to determine whether her cancer had spread. It had spread from her right hip to her breast to her lungs.

We now switch the scene of tragic human dramas from San Francisco today to the region around the Sea of Galilee in northern Palestine two thousand years ago. Jesus was on his way to the house of Jairus, one of the leaders of the synagogue, who had pleaded with Jesus to come and cure his daughter who was at the point of death (Mark 5:21–24). A large crowd was following him and pressing in on him (5:31). Everyone in the crowd was excited, and no one noticed a woman trying timidly and secretly to approach him. Who was she? We do not know. But we do know one thing about her illness. She

had been suffering from hemorrhages for twelve years [and] had endured much under many physicians, and had spent all that she had; and she was no better, but rather grew worse. She had heard about Jesus, and came up behind him in the crowd and touched his cloak, for she said, "If I but touch his clothes, I will be made well." (5:25–28).

What is the hemorrhage from which the woman was suffering for twelve years? It was "any bleeding or flow of blood visible or concealed, profuse or sporadic."[4] When the hemorrhage comes from a woman's body, it becomes a religious as well as physiological matter, certainly more religious than physiological in Jesus' time. As it is described in Leviticus in

3. *Alicia's Story* in six chapters is the personal account by Alicia Parlette and appeared in *San Francisco Chronicle* in series from June 5 to June 11, 2005. The excerpts of the story made here are from "Alicia's Story" published in *San Francisco Chronicle*.

4. Buttrick, *Interpreter's Dictionary of the Bible*, Volume 2., 581a-b.

the Hebrew Bible, "if a woman has a discharge of blood for many days, not at the time of her impurity, or if she has a discharge beyond the time of her impurity, all the days of the discharge she shall continue in uncleanness . . ." (Lev 15:25). What is described here is clearly a medical condition, but it was regarded to "bring with it ceremonial defilement, thus imposing serious restrictions upon the individual's religious and social life."[5]

Her physical suffering was great, and it was compounded by the religious law against it. For twelve years she suffered not only her medical condition but also the religious taboo related to her hemorrhage. That made her a religious and social outcast, barred from public worship and social contacts. She sought out physicians, but some of them, taking advantage of her condition, exploited her, leaving her helpless and impoverished. It is in this state of desperation that she mingled with the crowd to seek a cure from Jesus as the last resort without being noticed by anyone.

Alicia, in contrast, does not have to endure being religiously and socially ostracized because of her cancer. She was surrounded by her loving father and her caring friends. She was in the hands of competent doctors and nurses who applied the best tests and treatments medical science could give her to improve her condition. And there is something else for her other than her loving father, caring friends, and competent doctors. There is her faith in the all loving, all caring and all competent God! In the midst of her pain, suffering, doubt and distress, she is reminded that her family "went through the trials of my mom's cancer and stayed intact," that "they have no doubts in me and about what will happen because God and my mom are up there, working their everyday magic." She repeats to herself: "I am a miracle. I am a miracle. I am a miracle." And she writes:

> All of a sudden, I was out of the tunnel, looking out as the sun sneaked through Oakland's clouded sky. It sounds like a cliché, but it made me think of the trials we go through. They're uncomfortable and scary and dark and overwhelming—but then they're through, and things go back (almost) to normal, and God's back to showing himself on the other side. And he was never really gone, just up above, and all around, and even in a tunnel under a scary bay, helping frightened women come up with mantras.

5. Ibid., 581b.

Faith is a miracle, not faith in success, prosperity, and fame, but faith in God, above all, faith in God' presence through thick and thin.

Alicia finds herself praying to God, surrounded by the prayers of her dearest family members and friends:

> And Lord, thank you for giving me two of the best examples of
> how to go through this: Jesus Christ, who is the ultimate example
> of grace through suffering, and my mom, who is my favorite an-
> gel, who showed me that people can be divine here on earth.

This is a prayer from the heart, a prayer not centered on oneself, but on Jesus, "the ultimate example of grace through suffering," a prayer that turns its focus from one's self to God's grace in Jesus' suffering. To be able to say such a prayer in the midst of extreme pain and suffering is a miracle.

This must also be the prayer that the woman who suffered hemor-rhages for twelve years said when she mingled among the crowd. "If I but touch his clothes," she said as she tried to reach Jesus, surrounded by a thick and excited crowd, "I will be well." This was her prayer, a prayer from her heart, one that turns its focus from herself to God's grace active in Jesus. This prayer of hers was her faith, which would bring her the miracle of healing, but more importantly would make her a miracle, just as Alicia's faith made her a miracle.

The woman could not hide herself as a miracle any longer. For a miracle is a public event. She had to give up her anonymity and respond-ed in the hearing of the crowd to Jesus' question: "Who touched me?" (Mark 5:31). She, "in fear and trembling," had to respond to the question and said it was she who had touched him. She was expecting a repri-mand, even worse a punishment by Jesus of taking back the healing, leaving her to continue in her pain and suffering. But what she heard was entirely different. "Daughter," she heard Jesus say, "your faith has made you well; go in peace, and be healed of your disease" (5:34).

Your faith has made you well! Not my power of healing but your faith! Not my ability as a faith-healer but your faith! Not what some people say about me as the son of God, but your faith! That faith of hers in God is the life God gave her and each one of us when God not only created the heavens and the earth, but each and every living creature, each and every human being. What Jesus does is to activate that life God has given to us. Jesus is not a miracle worker, but an activator of the life

God has made. Jesus is not a magician, but an energizer who restores the energy of life in us that has been diminished by disease, pain, and suffering.

The woman with hemorrhages had to wait twelve years before she met Jesus. Alicia's life has become a life of waiting ever since she was diagnosed with cancer. This is what she tells us:

> So much of my life had become about waiting. I was waiting to see what the interferon would do, waiting until the fall to get more scans, waiting to see how my health would hold up . . .

But it was not a passive but an active waiting. She took part in a walk/run in Marin County for the Sarcoma Alliance, a non-profit group to help sarcoma patients. "Near the finish line," she writes,

> I sped up until I could feel the air flying past my face, until my feet were gliding across the trail without effort. I was running, really running. I zoomed past some walkers and, with a final burst, darted to the finish. My heart was pounding, I was sweaty, and I was the happiest I'd been in months. [She was presented] a picture frame with a mat border that said: "Running for Miracles" May 28, 2005.

Alicia is still waiting, actively waiting, to use her own words, "as I carry on with my life with faith and hope—with the love of so many holding me high . . ."

One does not wait until the end for a miracle to happen. Alicia's story tells us that life itself is a miracle, even a life wracked with pain, suffering and anxiety. Life consists of many miracles, miracles of waiting in faith and hope, of believing and experiencing God's grace. Faith does not do away with pain and suffering, but it does enable us to wait actively in hope, to walk in hope and even run in hope. Faith and hope in God do make Alicia's story and the story of the woman two thousand years ago interweave, becoming a tapestry of faith and hope. Does not each story of faith and hope in human history leave a mark on this tapestry that God alone will finish for us? And each story of faith and hope interwoven in the tapestry may be yours and mine also.

SIN AND DEATH

With birth, life begins, and with death life ends. It sounds very simple. But as we all know, the process from birth to death is anything but simple. It is so complex that many stories have been told and retold to come to grips with the mystery of it all. And most religions, although different one from each other in what they believe and teach, and how they practice faith, ultimately offer wisdom on life and death, especially on death. The central theme of religions, as in many stories, is life and death, particularly death.

There are two basic questions concerning death. Why do human beings have to die? This is the first question. The second question is: What might be done to overcome death? It is around these two questions that many folk stories have been created.

What is folk story as a genre? We will start with this question. *Folklore,* or *folk story,* "is a vivid record of a people, palpitating with life itself, and its greatest art is its artlessness. It is a true and unguarded portrait, for where art may be selective, may conceal, gloss over defects and even prettify, folk art is always revealing, always truthful in the sense that it is a spontaneous expression. It is therefore three-dimensional with 'life' and 'people.' . . . By juxtaposing good with evil, light with shadow, grief with laughter, and honesty with sham, it achieves the harmonious unity of opposites that resides in objective truth."[6]

Folk story is the people's story. It is a *vivid portrayal* of how people live, believe and go through life in hope and despair. It *reveals* what people harbor in the depths of their hearts, be it joy or sorrow, expectation or anxiety, confidence or fear, in everyday life and more importantly in life beyond death. It is *truthful* not in the sense that it is derived from what is called "objective truth," but because it gives expression to their genuine fear about things beyond their control and their sense of helplessness when faced with crises of life. It paints idealized pictures of the world of happiness and joy, but underneath is the world of the pain and agony created by evil, darkness, grief, and death. It asks why life and the world are full of pain and agony, grief and death. Is this not a mockery of the world without pain, agony, grief and death that God created?

Death in the Garden

The question just raised leads us to the third chapter of Genesis in the Hebrew Bible. What we have there is a story, or a narrative if you like, about the inevitable fact of life—death that puts an end to life. It is a folk

---

6. See Mintz, "Introduction," in Ausubel, *A Treasury of Jewish Folklore,* xxv.

tale, a story of people who had to witness firsthand the death inflicted on those around them and who had the premonition that the same fate would strike them sooner or later. What could express their helplessness in the face of death other than the touching words towards the end of the story. Those words say it all:

> . . . you are dust,
> and to dust you shall return. (Gen 3:19)

Death in the Garden! Not just any garden, but the Garden of Eden, "a well-watered, beautiful and fruitful area, a land of plenty, the land of bliss!"[7]

The folk story in Genesis 3 is addressed to "the subject matter . . . of universal interest and extent" about which "there are stories the world over."[8] One of the folk stories told about death the world over is called "And How Did It Happen?" from the Akamba tribe of Africa. It begins in this way:

> It is God who created human beings. And since God had pity, He said, "I do not wish human beings to die altogether. I wish that human beings, having died, should rise again." And so God created human beings and placed them in another region. But God stayed at home.[9]

In this African folktale, human beings are created by God just as in the creation story in Genesis 2. It tells us that "God does not wish human beings to die." Does this not say what the story in Genesis implies when it has God "breathed into their nostrils the breath of life" (Gen 2:7)? How could God wish human beings, into whom God breathed the breath of life, to die? But this African folktale presupposed that death is a fact of life, just as the Genesis story does when it says that human beings, having been taken out of the dust of the ground, are to return to dust. What does God have to do? What do human beings wish God to do? The African folktale comes up with an answer: God wishes that "human beings, after having died, should rise again." Here again God takes the initiative. After all, if creation is what God has taken the initiative to do, so is the matter of life and death. Does not God plant "the tree of life" in the garden (2:9)?

7. Westermann, *Genesis 1–11*, 193.

8. Ibid., 190.

9. This African folktale is found in Cole, *Best-Loved Folktales*, 631.

The African folktale goes on to tell us that God "placed human beings in another region." It does not, like the Genesis story, describe what this region is like, but it does remind us of "the garden in Eden God planted to put the human beings God had formed" (2:8), "a well-watered, beautiful and fruitful area [or region or garden], a land of plenty, the land of bliss."[10]

Here the similarities of images end between the Genesis story and the African folktale. For in the Genesis story, it is unthinkable that God has to do with human death. Adam and Eve are solely responsible for death because they disobeyed God by eating the forbidden fruit in the garden (Gen 3:1–7).The African folktale takes a different approach, almost a humorous or lighthearted tack. Isn't there some wisdom in taking on death with humor and lightheartedness? God speaks to the Chameleon, an honest and intelligent creature:

> "Chameleon, go into that region where I have placed the human beings I created, and tell them that when they have died, even if they are altogether dead, still they shall rise again—that each person shall rise again after he/she dies." The Chameleon said, "Yes, I will go." But he went slowly, for it is his fashion to go slowly . . .
>
> The chameleon traveled on, and when he had arrived at his destination, he said, "I was told, I was told, I was told. . . ." But he did not say what he had been told.
>
> The weaver-bird said to God, "I wish to step out for a moment." And God said to him, "Go!" But the bird, since he is a bird, flew swiftly, and arrived at the place where the chameleon was speaking to the people and saying, "I was told. . . ." Everyone was gathered there to listen. When the weaver-bird arrived, he said, "What was told to us? Truly, we were told that human beings, when they are dead, shall perish like the roots of the aloe."
>
> Then the chameleon exclaimed, "But we were told, we were told, we were told, that when human beings are dead, they shall rise again." Then the magpie interposed and said, "The first speech is the wise one."
>
> And now all the people left and returned to their homes. This was the way it happened. And so human beings become old and die; they do not rise again.[11]

---

10. Westermann, *Genesis 1–11*, 209.

11. "And How Did It Happen?" in Cole, *Best-Loved Folktales*, 631–32.

God has done all that God could to prevent the tragedy of death, only to end in failure. Is this not also what the story of the Garden of Eden in Genesis 3 insinuates?

Death is an anomaly of life, an irony of faith, and an absurdity to humanity. It is not God's intention for human beings to die. All living creatures die, but not human beings. All that is born has to die, but not you and I. Are not you and I, unlike other living things, "the apple of God's eye"? We are specially made by God to last a long, long time, even to all eternity. Is it not for this reason that "God formed human beings out of the dust of the ground, and breathed into their nostrils the breath of life" (2:7)? It is true that God formed human beings out of the dust of the ground, a perishable material, but the breath of life from God should have turned that perishable material into an imperishable substance, that mortal stuff into immortal essence. Does not death then negate what God has done? Does it not undo what God has done? Does not death prove to be more powerful than God when it turns human beings back to dust and takes away God's breath of life from us? Death makes an end of us. It is already frightful, but it is even more frightful when it seems able to make an end of God.

Throughout the history of humankind, human beings have tried to accept death as something natural, something we share with all things in nature, even with nature itself, regulated by the cycles of spring, summer, autumn and winter, the cycles of day and night. But for most of us death is not a natural thing. We are not supposed to be a natural thing, although we are, in a true sense, part of nature. We may be part of nature in many other things, but not in the thing called death. Did not the Apostle Paul, of all people, speak of death as "the last enemy to be destroyed" (1 Cor 15:26)? Did he not paraphrase the prophet Isaiah and declare stoically:

> Death has been swallowed up in victory.
> Where, O death, is your victory?
> Where, O death, is your sting? (15:54–55)

The Apostle Paul is talking about Jesus' resurrection. He is elated by his faith in the resurrection. But the fact of the matter is that Jesus did die on the cross, that human beings, whether they believe in Jesus' resurrection or not, die. Death has not been swallowed up in victory. It continues to have victory over us. It does not cease to sting us human beings.

"Have You Eaten from the Tree?"

That death is inevitable, that even human beings in whom God breathed the breath of life are mortal, is one of the central themes of the story in Genesis 3 and the African folktale "How Did It Happen?" It is fate; death is our fate. The Apostle Paul believes it is not fate because of faith in the resurrection. But there is still the question about the origin of death. If human beings are created by God, and it is God who has placed human beings in the Garden of Eden, in the region of eternal bliss, why do they have to die? How did death come about? What is the origin of death? God who created life cannot be its originator. If God is not the originator, who would that be except human beings themselves? The spearhead is thus pointed at human beings.

But what did human beings do to deserve death? Why did death intrude into human life and defeat it? The story of Genesis 3 addresses the question with a straightforward answer: the sin of disobeying upon God's command not to eat from the tree of the knowledge of good and evil (Gen 2:9). Did not God warn in advance that "of the tree of the knowledge of good and evil you shall not eat, for in the day that you eat of it you shall die" (2:17)? Death is not instituted by God; it is brought about by the human sin of disobedience to God's command. This point is dramatized by the storyteller, who has God ask Adam and Even: "Have you eaten from the tree of which I commanded you not to eat?" (3:11). The whole story is ingeniously crafted to lead to this point that the sinful party in the whole tragic affair is human beings and not God. This is the pivot of the story from which one reads back to the offense committed by human beings against God and reads forward to the divine punishment of death meted out to them.

Death is the price human beings have to pay for the sin of the betrayal they committed against God. As the Apostle Paul is to teach later, taking the story of Genesis 3 literally, "the wages of sin is death" (Rom 6:23). Death is therefore not so much a natural happening as a religious breach. It is the penalty human beings have to pay for not being content to be what they are and to be law-abiding people. This is how the Apostle Paul understands the meaning of death and what most religions teach about death. It is from this that the Apostle Paul, Christianity, and most of the other religions have developed ways of absolution from sin, to overcome death and to regain a life that is never to be threatened by death again.

There are "folktales the world over" that human beings are to blame for their sin as betrayal of God's trust in them. A folktale from Indonesia called "The Stone and the Banana" sheds an interesting light on how human beings wrestle with the never-ending search for the origin of death.

> Thus the natives of Poso, a district of Central Celebes, say that in the beginning the sky was very near the earth, and that the Creator, who lived in it, used to let down his gifts to human beings at the end of a rope. One day God thus lowered a stone; but our first father and mother would have none of it and they called out to their Maker, "What have we to do with this stone? Give us something else." The Creator complied and hauled away at the rope; the stone mounted up and up until it vanished from sight. Presently the rope was seen coming down from heaven again, this time there was a banana at the end of it instead of a stone. Our first parents ran at the banana and took it. Then there came a voice from heaven saying: "Because ye have chosen the banana, your life shall be like its life. When the banana-tree has offspring, the parent stem dies; so shall ye die and your children shall step into your place. Had ye chosen the stone, your life would have been like the life of the stone changeless and immortal." The man and his wife mourned over their fatal choice, but it was too late; that is how through the eating of a banana death came into the world.[12]

"It was too late"! Infinite regret and sadness are packed into these few words. Watching how death has taken away our dear ones, not one of us could conceal deep sorrow, saying in our hearts: "It was too late." The most fatal thing about death is that for human beings it is always too late; there is nothing that can be done about it. No power on earth can reverse it. There is this helpless feeling of finality to it. The question that grips us is always the same: How did death come about? What is the origin of it?

This Indonesian folktale, dealing with the sober subject of death, is a little frivolous and lighthearted like the African folktale of "How Did It Happen?" we have discussed. There is always this quality of frivolity and lightheartedness in folktales from Asia and Africa, a quality not so apparent in Western folktales. Perhaps this is one of the most effective ways to deal with sober subjects such as death. Since one cannot do anything about it, one may as well laugh at it, disguising the deep feelings of helplessness and vulnerability.

12. See Eliade, *From Primitives to Zen*, 140.

God does not leave human beings to sink or swim after creating them. God cares for them with gifts to sustain their life. God in this Indonesian folktale is the Creator as well as the Provider. Does not the creation story in the Hebrew Bible talk about God in the same way? Does not the Christian church teach about God as Creator and Provider? Originally the gift from God is a stone, a changeless and immortal stone. By sending our first parents this gift of a changeless and immortal stone, God intends human beings to be changeless and immortal too. Is this not also why God planted "the tree of life in the midst of the garden" in the Genesis story (Gen 2:9)?

Unfortunately, however, our first parents did not realize that the changeless and immortal quality of the stone was intended to make them changeless and immortal. What they saw was a hard stone not suitable to eat. This is the opposite of "the tree of the knowledge of good and evil" (Gen 2:9), the tree that was "good for food and a delight to the eyes" (3:6). The first ancestors in the Genesis story could not resist the temptation to eat from the tree. Our first parents in the Indonesian folktale they were repulsed by the stone and did not hide their displeasure from God. Tempted to eat from the tree or refusing to eat the stone, the consequence was equally disastrous. Human beings lost their immortality.

The concluding scenario of the Genesis story is as passionate as it is poignant. It tells us that God, very much alarmed, says almost frantically, "See, human beings have become like one of us . . . and now they might reach out their hand and take also from the tree of life, and eat, and live forever" (Gen 3:22). Something drastic had to be done. "Therefore," the story goes, "the Lord God drove human beings from the garden of Eden . . . and at the east of the garden of Eden God placed the cherubim, and a sword flaming and turning to guard the way to the tree of life" (3:23–24). What a dreadful sight, human beings driven out of the garden of eternal bliss in tears and remorse and angels turning flaming swords to guard the gate of the garden, barring human beings' return to it forever. This may make a good religious painting, but for human beings the loss of eternal life is final and irredeemable.

Our first parents in the Indonesian folktale fare no better. By rejecting the stone of changelessness and immortality and "ran at the banana and took it," they also made a fateful choice. Their "life shall be like the life of a banana," temporal and transient. When they realized the calamitous mistake they had committed, "it was too late." And the Indonesian folktale concludes with almost the same desolate and bleak tone as the

Genesis story, saying, "that is how through the eating of a banana death came into the world."

TRANSFORMATION

Is death, then, the end of life? Is it the termination of who we are and what we are? Is it the finale of all that we do? Is it the end beyond which nothing exists? Is human life like "the epiphyllum blooming at night and disappearing in the morning" (*tan hua yi shian* in Chinese)? Even epiphyllum will bloom again when the next year comes round, but human beings? Once death occurs, there is no next year. Time is frozen, with all that is related to it. Many folktales, however, do not leave us human beings in the clutch of death. They seek to defrost the time that is frozen, to reopen the frontier of a new life not controlled by death. It is not uncommon, therefore, to come across folktales that explore the new frontiers of life beyond death, a new realm of life not dictated by death, and to envision a Garden of Eden or a region of eternal bliss once lost to human beings. It is no wonder that the theme of transformation of life, following the theme of sin and death, is pursued with great rigor and vivid imagination in most religions and folktales.

"Take, this is my body"

It is a very somber occasion. Jesus, his disciples and followers are gathered in a room in Jerusalem to eat the Passover meal, remembering and celebrating how God liberated their ancestors from slavery in Egypt many, many centuries ago. Those present in the room dream of liberation from Roman colonial rule. They expect a leader, anointed by God, a messiah, to lead them in the restoration of the kingdom their revered King David some three thousand years ago had established. But Jesus has a different dream. He has a dream of transforming death into life, of transition from the temporal life to eternal life, converting life on earth to life with God.

Jesus alone knows his death by crucifixion is imminent. But he is preoccupied more with life than with death. The cross is a cruel punishment imposed on the enemies of the Roman Empire. How is his violent death to be transformed into God's affirmation of life? With words and actions he enacts the great story of his passion that later is told in the Gospels. At the heart of this story is what Jesus did with the bread and the wine. He

> took a loaf of bread, and after giving blessing it he broke it, and gave it to them, and said, "Take; this is my body." Then he took a cup, and after giving thanks he gave it to them, and all of them drank from it. He said to them, "This is my blood of the covenant, which is poured out for many." (Mark 14:22–24)[13]

With these words of Jesus, the bread that he gave the disciples to eat is transformed into his body, and the wine he gave them to drink is changed into his blood. The bread is still bread, but it *is* Jesus' body; the wine is still wine, but it *is* now Jesus' blood.

The story Jesus enacted through these words has this astounding power of transformation. It transforms matter into spirit; it transforms human tragedy to the divine "comedy"; it transforms the most brutal form of execution into the compassion of God's saving love. And it transforms death into life. Another word for this "substantial" transformation, transformation not just of an external form but transformation of the substance, the essence, that makes the form possible, is *resurrection*. Is this not what underlies what the women who had come from Galilee with Jesus (Luke 23:55) heard at Jesus' tomb? This is what they heard: "Why do you look for the living among the dead? He is not here, but has risen" (24:5).

It has to be this transformation that we celebrate at the Lord's Supper. At the Lord's Supper we remember that Jesus before the night of his arrest ate his last meal with his disciples and followers. We remember how he suffered and died on the cross. But more importantly, at the Lord's Supper we celebrate the transformation of bread into Jesus' body and wine into his blood, transformation of the death on the cross into the resurrection of life from the tomb, transformation of an old life destroyed by death into a new life re-created by God.

Is such transformation nothing but a myth? Is it "mythological"? Does not what we have in the Gospels in the New Testament anything but daydreaming caused by the extreme anguish of Jesus' death? Is not such a life, life beyond the grip of death, life liberated from death, what is called resurrection life, anything but wishful thinking? This prompts us to ask what myth is and requires us to reinstate myth not only as a genre, but as part of the real life we live in eternity as well as in time. This we have to do before going any further.

---

13. Also Matt 26:28 and Luke 22:17–20.

What is *myth*, then? "Myth," it is explained, "is a story—usually of unknown origins—by which culture attempts to express its origins, its place in the universe, and/or its sense of identity and purpose. . . . Myths are stories that are literally or symbolically true to particular cultures and that contain elements in which outsiders with open minds can find archetypal or universal truths. In this latter sense, myths can be said to be the cultural vehicles for understandings that people in all corners of the world have shared."[14] What is said about myth here ought to redress whatever misunderstanding and misgiving we have had about myth.

Myth is a story that can be close or remote to the reality of life.[15] Even when it is remote to the reality of life, it originated in life, and as time goes on, it gets removed more and more from its original reality and takes on "mythological," that is, unreal, attributes, creating illusions. This often happens to myths created by authoritarian rulers to intimidate people and fortify their power. As a matter of fact, this anomaly does not occur only to myths; it occurs to all genres of stories. For this reason it is important, as we deal with stories theologically, to identify as much as possible the situations that give rise to particular stories. We will return to this point in our next and last chapter as we discuss the methods of doing story theology.

Apart from politics, religion is a potent source of myths. In a sense, religion is a myth-making factory, producing good and bad myths. "Religions," it is pointed out, "of course, are concerned with ritual, theology, and other elements as well as myth, but myths are the sacred stories of religion, the narratives are used to support, explain, or justify rituals, theology, ethics, and so forth."[16] It is in this sense of myth as "the sacred stories of religion" that we want to explore the meaning of transformation in the following verses from the Rig Veda.

14. Leeming, *Dictionary of Asian Mythology*, 13.

15. In the "Digest" section of *San Francisco Chronicle*, July 25, 2005, A4, a short article under the title, "Myths may be rooted in fact, study says," begins with these words: "Traditional stories of epic battles and two-headed monsters told by American Indians of the North-west may have their roots in historic earthquakes, a University of Washington researcher suggests."

16. Leeming, *Dictionary of Asian Mythology*, 2.

"We Have Drunk Soma, Have Become Immortal"

The Rig Veda is part of the most ancient of Indian scriptures basic to Hinduism and believed to be inspired by God.[17] The poetic form in which the following prayer is cast reflects the transformation we discussed earlier. This prayer is called "We Have Drunk Soma, Have Become Immortal":

> We have drunk soma, have become immortal,
> Gone to the light have we, the gods discovered.
> What can hostility do against us?
> What, O Immortal, mortal man's fell purpose?
>
> Joy to our heart be thou, when drunk, O Indu,
> Like father to a son, most kind, O Soma;
> Thankful like friend to friend, O thou of wide fame,
> Prolong our years that we may live, O Soma.
>
> These glorious freedom-giving drops by me imbibed
> Have knit my joints together as straps a chariot;
> From broken legs may Soma drops protect me,
> May they from every illness keep me far removed. . . .
>
> Be gracious unto us for good, King Soma;
> We are thy devotees; of that be certain.
> When might and wrath display themselves, O Indu,
> Do not abandon us, as wished by foemen.
>
> Protector of our body art thou, Soma,
> In every limb hast settled man-beholding:
> If we infringe thine ordinances be gracious
> As our good friend, O god, for higher welfare. . . .
>
> Ailments have fled away, diseases vanished,
> The powers of darkness have become affrighted.
> With might hath Soma mounted up within us;
> The dawn we've reached, where human beings renew Existence.
> . . .
>
> Uniting with the Fathers hast thou, Soma,
> Thyself extended over earth and heaven.
> Thee, Indu, would we worship with oblation,
> And we ourselves become the lords of riches.[18]

17. The Veda consists of four collections called the Rig Veda, Yajur Veda, Sama Veda and Atharva Veda, the oldest of which may date from 1500 BCE.

18. From Eliade, *From Primitives to Zen*, 246–47.

This can be said to be the Rig Veda's sacramental hymn, praying for the transformation of mortal life into life immortal. Does not this ancient hymn of India remind us of the Last Supper at which Jesus spiritually and symbolically transformed the bread and wine into his own body and blood, envisioning an eternal life in God through his death on the cross?

"*Soma*" plays a prominent role in the hymn. What is *soma*? "Derived from the Sanskit root meaning 'to press' . . . *soma* was a drink pressed from a type of mushroom called *soma*." It was "personified and worshipped as the god Soma in the ancient Indian Vedas. The god Soma was a source of imaginative power much praised in the *Rig Veda*." How is the drink *soma* made, and how does it possess the power of transforming mortal human beings into immortal? The Vedic priests "pressed the *soma* plant, extracting the sacred essence . . . If consumed, it would bring remarkable insights. If placed in the ritual fire as a sacrifice, it would rise up to gods in the smoke and become their ambrosia of immortality and the source of their power."[19]

The process of making the drink called *soma* resembles that of wine made from grapes. When used in religious rituals, wine is first transformed into the sacred substance that brings about transformation in the believers who drink it. In the Lord's Supper, the bread and wine are "transformed" (or "transubstantiated," as the Roman Catholic Church calls it) into the body and blood of Christ that have saving efficacy on those who partake of them. It is no wonder that in the medieval Roman Catholic Church the elements of the sacraments were revered as "medicine of eternal life" enabling believers to "partake in the mystery of the relationship between Christ and his church"[20] and the relationship between believers and God.

The Transfiguration of Jesus

The supreme concern of religion, any religion, is life, or to be more specific, transformation from impermanent life to permanent life, from transient life to lasting life, from temporal life to abiding life. We human beings are aware of the passing nature of life, but we are also aware that transience cannot fully explain the true nature of our life. If there is transience, there must be permanence. The life we live may pass away, but it

19. From Leeming, *Dictionary of Asian Mythology*, 63.
20. Elwell, *Evangelical Dictionary of Theology*, 965a.

does not pass away into nothing. If it does not pass away into nothing, it could not have come from nothing. Nothing, strictly speaking, is not nothing. For nothing to be nothing, there must be something. Likewise, life could not have come from nothing and return to nothing. It must have come from something and pass into something. What is this something that forms the substance of the life we live in time?

The question of life begins in this way in our experience of life, the life we live, each for a different length of time. This has been the case since the time of our ancestors millions of years ago, when they began to experience the time-bound reality of life. We human beings have therefore been telling real-life stories about life, about its joy and despair, its longing and fear. These stories are human quests for something that should have preceded the present life and something that should come after the present life. Since this is the quest that has no convincing answer here and now, they began to develop into folktales, fairy tales, legends, and eventually myths. Even they are evolved into a myth, what underlies the myth is the real-life story lived and experienced by a host of people.

The hymn of the Rig Veda was first dedicated to the drink *soma* specially concocted to bring about transformation of life. "We have drunk soma," intones the hymn, "have become immortal." A fantasy? An illusion? An intoxication? Yes, but it expresses an ardent prayer of the devotees for an immortal life, life not as a passing phenomenon but as eternal reality. This drink itself was transformed, in this Vedic hymn, into "King *Soma*, our Stengthener, our Protector and our Light-finder." What we have in this hymn from ancient India is the most primordial and at the same time perennial longing and experience of human beings to taste an immortal life in the life that is mortal and ephemeral.

This leads us to the story of Jesus' transfiguration in the New Testament (Mark 9:2–10).[21] As Mark tells us:

> Jesus took with him Peter and James and John, and led them up a high mountain apart, by themselves. And he was *transfigured*[22] before them, and his clothes became dazzling white, such as no one on earth could bleach them. And there appeared to them Elijah with Moses, who were talking with Jesus. . . . Then a cloud overshadowed them, and from the cloud there came a voice, "This is my Son, the Beloved, listen to him."

21. Also Matt 17:1–9 and Luke 9:28–36.

22. Italics added.

What a fantastic story! No, it is not a fantastic story; it is a wonderful story. Is this not a myth? Yes, it is a myth, but not a myth as people commonly understand it as something not real and fabricated; it is a myth reflecting the true story of what lies deeply in our soul and spirit, a story not of our self-transcendence, but a prototypical story of God transforming our temporal life into eternal life. Does this not remind us of what the Apostle Paul says in his first letter to the Christians at Corinth? He writes:

> Listen, I will tell you a mystery! We will not all die, but we will all be changed [transformed or transfigured], in a moment, in the twinkling of an eye, at the last trumpet. For the trumpet will sound, and the dead will be raised imperishable, and we will be changed [transformed or transfigured]. For this perishable body must put on imperishability, and this mortal body must put on immortality . . . (1 Cor 15:51–53)

Do we not hear the echo of what the Apostle Paul calls "mystery" in the ancient Vedic Hymn of India? And do we not hear the echo of this "mystery" in the story of Jesus' transfiguration on a high mountain?

"Why Do You Look for the Living among the Dead?"

This change, this transfiguration and this transformation, is developed into the stories of Jesus' appearances to his women followers and his disciples.[23] As a story develops to this level, it cannot be contained in any genre or form, be it real story, legend, folktale, fairy tale, or myth. It is an *event*, but not an event that can fit into any of the genres or forms we discussed earlier. It is an event that happens deep in the spirit of a person who experiences it as a real event in one's life. It can also be told and retold as something real, certain and objective; that is why there are appearance stories in the Gospels, stories of the risen Jesus who appears to them. To those who believe, they are also deeply spiritual experiences. The community of believers is built on this spiritual encounter with the living Jesus. What the Apostle Paul says about the cross of Jesus can be equally true of the appearances of the risen Christ. To paraphrase Paul, the experience of Christ risen from death is "a stumbling block to Jews and foolishness to Gentiles, but to those who are called, both Jews

---

23. What are commonly known as stories of Jesus' resurrection in the Gospels are in fact stories of his appearances to his women followers and his disciples.

and Greeks, Christ is the power of God and the wisdom of God" (1 Cor 1:23–24). As a matter of fact, many stories from all over the world, from East to West, from South to North, try to deal with the human quest for a life beyond the grave. Life does not end at death; it reaches a dark night of death only to begin a life that never ends.

The stories of Jesus' appearances in the Gospels, seen in relation to the universal human quest for a lasting authentic life, give us more than glimpses of what that life may be like. As one of the appearance stories tells us (Luke 24:1–12)[24] the women who had followed Jesus from Galilee to Jerusalem came to Jesus' tomb early in the morning three days after Jesus' death on the cross. To their consternation they found the tomb empty. Now knowing what to do, they heard a voice say to them: "Why do you look for the living among the dead? He is not here, but has risen" (24:5).

These words seem innocent and well-intentioned. The women were in deep sorrow; they had to witness Jesus' death and burial. But these words find a way into the story here not merely to give them comfort, strength and hope. These words are a breakthrough in the universal human quest for a life not terminated by death, but a life born out of the womb of death. They should not be looking for the living among the dead. There is in fact no living among the dead; there is only the dead among the dead. They should be looking for the living among the living. The living could not be sealed in a tomb. That is why the tomb is empty; that is why they could not find the living Christ in the tomb. He is risen! He is as living as he had been when he was with them. He is in fact more living now that he is risen than when he was with them in flesh and blood. A stupendous transformation, an amazing transfiguration, has taken place. These women and later Jesus' disciples and other followers, came to realize the meaning of this transformation of life and its transfiguration, a life no longer in the grip of death, but a life that renders death meaningless.

This is what the women at Jesus' tomb realized. At first they were puzzled by what they had seen and heard, but then it dawned on them that Jesus was with them as the living Christ. They had no reason to tally at the tomb. They left it and "told all this to the eleven [disciples] and all the rest" (24:9). The story they told is the story of Jesus risen from the dead, the story of Jesus who lived and lives. This story of the living Christ

24. Also Matt 28:1–8.

goes all the way back to stories of human quests of the living among the dead; it also goes all the way forward to inspire all future stories in search of a life never to be touched by death. In this story of the women at Jesus' tomb, we have the most intense theology of life that interacts with all other stories wrestling with breakthrough to life from death. How is such intense theology to be born out of the matrix of stories? In the next and final chapter, we will engage ourselves with ways in which theology is to be grown out of interactions between the Bible and stories from sources other than the Bible.

10

The Bible, Stories, and Theology

THEOLOGY DOES NOT GROW on a plastic tree, nor does a religious faith, for that matter. Whether it is religious faith or theology that accounts for faith, faith and theology are not attached to a plastic tree as decorations are attached to a plastic Christmas tree. Christmas decorations are kept in a box and stored away. When Christmas comes round in December, a Christmas tree is assembled. Then Christmas decorations are taken out of the box in which they were stored a year ago and attached to the Christmas tree. What remains to be done is simply to turn on the lights, and voila! A lighted Christmas tree with all the decorations to give us the atmosphere of celebration and the joy of Christmas.

But theology is not attached to a plastic tree like Christmas decorations. It grows on a real tree with its roots deep down in the earth, branches stretching towards the sky and leaves giving vital signs of life. Theology grows from it, and not attached to it. It is a living part of the live tree, born with it, grows with it, and goes through all the vicissitudes of life with it.

What is this tree with which and from which theology grows? It is stories of all genres or forms, from current stories to legends to folktales, to fairy tales to myths. This should be clear now that we have reflected on stories from many different aspects and talked about them in many different settings. Our reflections have led us to the question of how stories in the Christian Bible and stories outside it can interact with one another for Christian theology to grow from the interactions. One may call this the "method" of doing story theology.

But *method* is a rather intimidating word; it is a constricting term also. It means ground rules and procedures one has to follow when one is engaged in story theology. It means guidelines and instructions set up in advance to regulate the ways in which one selects data and interprets them. That is why the question of method is usually discussed, clarified and decided at the outset of a theological treatise.

For us, however, consideration and reflection on method come at the end. Since it is our view that theology grows out of stories, we have, in the previous chapters, tried the best we could to come to grips with theological insights embedded in stories. Theology is an articulation of these theological insights already deposited in stories. We have now reached the stage of our efforts to look back on what we have done to deliberate how stories in the Bible and those outside it can impact one another, enabling theological visions to come out into the open. Instead of using the term "method," we would rather like to call what we are going to do here in this final chapter "approaches." We admit that there are other approaches to story theology, but the approaches that help us along the way are found to be most useful to us as we pursue theology conceived in stories, nurtured in them, and grow in them.

FIVE APPROACHES TO STORY THEOLOGY

A story is an abyss of meanings. Deep in that abyss is a universe of meanings. In stories universes of meanings converge. We use words such as *abyss* and *universe* to express what we have said earlier about "Stories within a Story" in chapter 7. If we believe that in stories God and human beings interact to create the spiritual as well the physical space for time and eternity, words such as *abyss* and *universe* help us appreciate the immense world of stories. In stories we are dealing with what it means to have faith, hope and love in a world of anxiety, despair and hostility. How do we, then, go about doing story theology? How do we penetrate that abyss of meanings to encounter the universe of meanings in which people from different cultures and religions echo one another's despairs and hopes?

There are at least five approaches to story theology. There may be more, but these five approaches are basic to those who endeavor to let stories speak with their own theological voices in their engagement with God, human beings and the world. Let us take these five approaches and discuss them one by one.

1. Story as Story Theology

A story is not simply a story; it is already a story theology, though not in an overt or conspicuous way. Here theology is used neither in the restricted sense of teachings and doctrines authorized by the church nor in the sense of conceptually developed systems of beliefs, premises and assertions made by theologians. Theology in "story as story theology" is coterminous with life, that is to say, life makes theology possible on the one hand and, on the other, it makes theology necessary. Theology depends on life for what it does. Separated from life, theology loses its ground and reason to be.

Life, of course, is inseparably related to God, at least to parts of who and what God is. The ancient Hebrew writers grasped this divine dimension of human nature with this profound statement: "God created humankind in God's image, in the image of God, God created them . . ." (Gen 1:27). Theology thus takes upon itself the task of explaining what it has perceived God to be and what God is doing in the lives of women, men, and children through the stories they live and tell.

It is evident that you cannot do story theology if you bypass stories. If you bypass stories, you are bypassing theology. But how do you penetrate the layers of stories to come to grips with the theological insights concealed in each layer of stories? What does one do to be moved and inspired by the men, women and children in the stories that search for ways to be human, to be united with the source of their life and being?

Awareness of the theological nature of stories is the first approach to story theology. What you need to do at this initial stage is to immerse yourself in the story by "reading it a hundred times so that its (theological) meaning may be disclosed to you" (*shu tu pai pian, ch'i yi zu chian*), to use a Chinese expression. It should be an attentive and intentional reading—attentive because in the story you are entering a world alien to your own world, an experience different from your own experience, and intentional because you are making conscious efforts to interact with the world and the experience of the story with your own.

Take, for example, the story of Job in the Hebrew Bible. You may have read it many times, if not a hundred times, but most likely not attentively or intentionally enough. You have read it with the conventional teaching about Job as a paragon of patience eventually to win God's approval and blessings after having survived his extreme suffering. But if you read the story over and over again attentively and intentionally, you would realize that Job is anything but a paragon of patience. In fact, he grows more and more impatient with his three friends who represent conventional faith and theology. He gets more and more suspicious of the official teaching on suffering as the sin one has committed openly or secretly. Finally, he has to take his case to God. Even there he does not get the answer to the problem of why he has had to suffer. What he has to do is to submit to the mercy of God the creator and redeemer who alone holds the key to the mysteries of life and world.

Reading the story of Job in this way is itself an engagement with story theology. You become immersed in the story. Job's problem becomes your problem. His impatience becomes your impatience, and his suffering your suffering. Just as Job, you are not likely to find answers to your agonizing questions about life and its adversities, but you will find yourself in the presence of the merciful God who takes all your agonies and sufferings into God's own boundless compassion. Here, instead of an answer, you find healing. This is what Job finally finds—the healing of his wounded soul in the embrace of the compassionate God.

2. Storytelling as Story Theology in Practice

You do story theology not only listening to stories; you are practicing it when you tell stories—stories of others, stories of the past, and above all, your own stories. Telling stories is another potent way of doing story theology.

It is potent because, first of all, you are exposed to the powers that fetter humanity. We all know that history consists of stories, stories of rulers and the ruled, of victimizers and victims, of masters and slaves, of victors and the defeated, of glory to some, and of suffering to the majority of others. A Chinese idiom expresses it well when it says: "one general achieves renown over the dead bodies of ten thousand soldiers" (*yi chiang kong cheng wan ku khu*).

The saying conjures up in our mind's eye a startlingly contrasting picture: on the one hand a victorious general leading his troops back to the capital receiving all the adulations of the excited crowds lining the streets to welcome him home, and, on the other, the eerily quiet battlefield on which thousands of uniformed soldiers lay dead. Do these wardead have stories to tell? Or would their stories follow them to the grave never to be told? Is it not said that "the dead have no mouth"? But these wardead and those who died at the hands of their fellow human beings have stories to tell, endless stories to tell. They tell their stories through their lifeless bodies and their tightly closed lips, and they tell their stories through the mouths of others who are moved and touched by their stories.

The stories of the victims of the Nazi atrocity in Europe during World War II are told, for example, by a young Jew who survived the Holocaust. This is what he tells us:

> Never shall I forget that night in camp, which gas turned my life into one long night, seven times cursed and seven times sealed. Never shall I forget the smoke. Never shall I forget the little faces of the children, whose bodies I saw turned into wreaths of smoke beneath a silent blue sky. Never shall I forget those flames which consumed my faith forever. Never shall I forget that nocturnal silence which deprived me, for all eternity, of the desire to live. Never shall I forget those moments which murdered my God and my soul and turned my dreams to dust. Never shall I forget these things, even if I am condemned to live as long as God Himself. Never.[1]

"Never shall I forget"! We tell stories because "we shall not forget." Stories are stored in our memories, and it is storytellers who turn the memories of the dead into stories so that those who are dead can continue to tell their stories.

By telling the story of the Holocaust, the author of *Night* is also doing theology. In those words quoted above, he is already doing so much theology—theology of human nature and destiny, theology of evil committed by human beings who are themselves created in God's image, and theology on God, asking whether it is still possible to believe in God after such unimaginable crimes against humanity and what kind of God could continue to command human faith. He is doing story theology in earnest, in perplexity and in agony, wanting to cling to faith in the God believed to be the creator and redeemer.

The author of *Night* takes us to the eve of Rosh Hashanah, the last day of the year, celebrated in a concentration camp. "They gave us our evening meal," he tells us, "a very thick soup, but no one touched it. We wanted to wait until after prayers. At the place of assembly, surrounded by electrified barbed wire, thousands of silent Jews gathered, their faces

---

1. Words of Elie Wiesel, quoted by Mauriac in his "Introduction" to Wiesel, *Night,* ix.

stricken. . . . Night was falling. Other prisoners continued to crowd in, from every block. . . ." In the midst of muted agony, he found himself angrily debating with God in his mind:

> What are You, my God, compared to this afflicted crowd, pro-claiming to You their faith, their anger, their revolt? What does your greatness mean, Lord of the universe, in the face of all this weakness, this decomposition, and this decay? Why do you still trouble their sick minds, their crippled bodies?[2]

If this is not theology, what is? If storytelling is not theology, what is? If engaging with God through telling stories out of the abyss of suffering and doubt is not theology, what is? There is more than enough in these words for biblical and dogmatic theologians to wrestle with in their whole lifetime, even more than their whole lifetime. As a matter of fact, their theology becomes pale and weak when confronted with such powerful questions from the abyss of senselessness seeking in vain a universal answer.

Do not these searching and agonizing words take us back to the cross planted outside Jerusalem in the place called Golgatha two thousand years ago? On that cross hangs Jesus in the throes of death. And from the mouth of the dying Jesus these words burst out, haunting not only those who put him there, not only those jeering him, not only the women at the foot of the cross crying their hearts out, but men and women in the past two thousand years and today who try to make sense of that great tragedy: "My God, my God, why have your forsaken me?" (Mark 15:34)[3] Two thousand yeas separate the story of the Holocaust survivor and the story of Jesus' death on the cross, but the most fundamental question unites them, the question of why God forsakes innocent people.

But time moves on and the horror of World War II and the Holocaust are behind us. It is now "twenty-five years after, a quarter century" from those horrible years.

> And we pause, trying to find bearings, trying to understand: what and how much did these years mean? To some a generation, to others an eternity. A generation without eternity. Children con-demned never to grow old, old men [and women] doomed never

2. Wiesel, *Night*, 63.
3. Also Matt 27:46.

to die. A solitude engulfing entire peoples, a guilt tormenting all humanity. A despair that found a face but not a name. A memory cursed, yet refusing to pass on its curse and hate. An attempt to understand, perhaps even to forgive. That is a generation. Ours.[4]

Plenty of theology is loaded into these words. It is a theology of under-standing—understanding the meaning of history and eternity, under-standing bad memories and divine forgiveness, understanding relations between God and humanity. In this story the storyteller is engaged in story theology as he seeks to understand what God is doing or not do-ing. Is this not the story of Jesus' cross? Is not the story of Jesus' cross the supreme story theology?

3. Story Theology as Empathetic Response to Stories

Stories are told to be responded to. Storytelling is not the monologue of a storyteller. It is a dialogue between the storyteller and the story listener. It is more than a dialogue. The story told is not just a medium, a means, an avenue. It becomes the story of the storyteller and it also becomes the story of the story listener. From someone else's story it becomes *my* story of the storyteller and *your* story of the story listener. From my story and your story it then becomes *our* story.

Likewise, it takes more than one person to do theology. Even God alone cannot do theology; God needs human beings and other things in nature to be God. That is why in the beginning were creation stories, and these creation stories continue to unfold themselves in human lives, in the history of peoples and nations. "God's word," to paraphrase the words in the prologue of John's Gospel (1:14), "become stories and lived among us."

If God cannot be alone as God, it is even more so for us human beings. Human beings need God to be able to do theology. They also need each other to be able to do theology. Furthermore, they need other things in God's universe to be able to do theology. Theology is a living enterprise. It is done by the living God, by living human beings, and by the animated creation. In telling stories and by listening to stories, we are engaged in story theology, trying to fathom the divine and human meanings deposited in layers of stories and above all in the depths of stories.

4. Wiesel, *One Generation After*, 3

One of the most brilliant story theologies is the Magnificat attributed to Mary, mother of Jesus. Although we already referred to it earlier, we need to bring it up again here in the context of our approaches to story theology. In Luke's account, Mary, when told that the Holy Spirit would come upon her and that she would give birth to a child (1:35), responded with the song of praise (the Magnificat), saying:

> My soul magnifies the Lord,
> and my spirit rejoices in God my Savior,
> for God has looked with favor
> on the lowliness of his servant.
> Surely, from now on
> all generations will call me blessed;
> for the Mighty One has done great things for me,
> and holy is God's name. . . .
> God has brought down the powerful from their thrones,
> and lifted up the lowly;
> God has filled the hungry with good things,
> and cast the rich away empty. . . . (Luke 1:46–55)

What makes Mary exultant is that God "has brought down the powerful from their thrones." This is also the experience of many people throughout history when they are freed from the tyranny of power held by emperors, dictators and autocratic rulers. That God "lifted up the lowly" makes Mary elated. Just think of the men and women who, treated as disposable things in a feudal society and under dictatorship, who have now regained dignity as human beings, and who carry out their duties and enjoy their rights in a democratic society! Even if they do not believe in the same God as Mary, even if their circumstances are different from Mary's, and even if they do not speak the same native language and the language of faith as Mary, they would surely resound from the bottom of their hearts Mary's song of praise when she sings in gratitude:

> My soul magnifies the Lord,
> and my spirit rejoices in God,
> for God has looked with favor
> on the lowliness of God's servant.
> Surely, from now on
> all generations will call me blessed;
> for the Mighty One has done great things for me,
> and holy is God's name. (Luke 1:46–49)

This is Mary's song of praise; it is the song of countless people set free from the incarceration of the body and the spirit. This is Mary's song of healing, healing from the extreme sorrow she felt as she watched her son die at the hands of those in power; it is also the song of healing for those who had their loved ones taken away and murdered by the Nazi police and soldiers who served at the beck and call of their cruel masters.

4. Doing Story Theology within a Renewing Community

Story is a community event, or communion happening. This should be crystal clear from our foregoing discourse. In fact it is the way it should be. From the moment of one's conception in her mother's womb to the moment of her departure from the world, no human being is an isolated and self-made individual.

You are conceived in the communion of your mother and father, brought into the world in a community of doctors and nurses. As you grow, your community of acquaintances and colleagues broadens and your communion of friends and loved ones deepens. Stories multiply in your broadening community and deepening communion. Stories, no matter which genre or form they may take, are community happenings and communion events. You are an individual person, yet you are not. You are a member of a family, a tribe, a people, a nation. It is in a community of people and communion of persons that your life is rooted and your stories take place, expand and multiply.

Your stories are your stories and yet not your stories only. Your stories are stories of your family, not only stories of your nuclear family, but stories of your extended family that includes generations of ancestors. Your stories are also stories of your people and your nation. But your stories do not stop there. Your stories are visibly and invisibly related to the great family of people before you, the people you would never know. When archaeologists and anthropologists build stories of people from the ancient past based on the bits and pieces of them discovered in Africa, for instance, these stories are also your stories. In this way your stories as an individual person stretch horizontally to interweave with the stories of others tens and hundreds of thousands of miles away; it also stretches vertically to intersect with the stories of those before you millions of years ago.

Stories in this way cross the boundaries of time and space to connect humanity scattered over all places and over all times. That is why stories in a particular place and at a particular time could be stories in other places and in other times. Stories have the capacity to transcend time and space, the capacity of which doctrines, canons of faith, creeds or ideologies are more likely to be in short supply. One may go so far as to say that while doctrines, canons of faith, creeds or ideologies divide people, stories unite them. We have, in the previous chapters, demonstrated that this is true.

Both doctrines and stories reorganize and realign people's loyalty and commitment. While doctrines tend to restrict reorganization and realignment, stories expand them. The communion and community of stories expand and extend, while those of doctrines harden and contract. Stories open people's hearts to one another in empathy; doctrines, however, inhibit believers to participate in the community and communion of stories. That is why stories compel participants to develop alternate life-views and worldviews, even to reconstruct their faith and conviction very differently from the faith and conviction authorized by their doctrinal traditions and religious conventions. Stories have this liberating power, the power that liberates people from their religious restrictions and doctrinal strictness, enabling them to meet one another and meet God in one another.

As an example, we refer to the at once marvelous and breathtaking stories towards the end of that often misused book called "Revelation" in the New Testament. These are the stories of Christians coping with sporadic Roman persecutions. John himself, the author the book, had just fled "the nails and teeth" (*jao ya* in Chinese) of Roman persecutors and found a refuge on a small island called Patmos in the Aegean Sea, about seven miles southeast of Miletus, a city in western Asia Minor. From there he wrote to the Christian communities anticipating serious persecutions to come. "I, John, your brother who share with you in Jesus the persecution and the kingdom and patient endurance, was on the island called Patmos because of the word of God and the testimony of Jesus" (Rev 1:9).

What follows are the stories of the Christian communities either struggling to survive the great ordeals of persecution or testifying to Jesus as their savior against all odds. The world in which they live and suffer is an old and decaying world. They anticipate a new world in which they can tell different stories, stories of joy instead of pain, stories of the life renewed and regenerated instead of the life subjected to decay and death. In telling stories in the old world of fear and suffering, they also tell stories of peace and joy in a new world.

Towards the end of the book, the story John is telling takes a surprising turn:

> Then I saw a new heaven and a new earth; for the first heaven and
> the first earth had passed away, and the sea was no more. . . . And
> I heard a loud voice from the throne saying,
> "See, the home of God is among mortals.
> He will dwell with them,
> they will be his peoples,
> and God himself will be with them;
> he will wipe away tear from their eyes.
> Death will be no more;
> mourning and crying and pain will be no more,
> for the first things have passed away." (21:1–4)

This is a community of God and human beings, a community renewed for new days. This is also a communion of God and peoples, a communion in which God communes with peoples and peoples commune with God.

What we have here in the book of Revelation are stories told in the everyday world of pain, suffering and death in anticipation of these stories transformed into stories of joy, peace and eternal life. Are not these stories a prime example of doing story theology in a community of persecuted Christians and in a communion of hope in eternal life? And do we not hear echoes of such stories told and told again in human communities of birth, old age, sickness and death in anticipation of communion with God and with one another in "a new heaven and a new earth" in which "God will wipe every tear from their eyes" and in which "death will be no more, mourning and crying and pain will be no more"?

Most tribes, peoples and nations undergo similar experiences of crisis, destruction and death to regain hope, renew their sense of unity as a community and reawaken their faith in the communion with a power greater than theirs. This is what religious festivals all over the world and throughout the ages do for their believers to attain spiritual well-being in the life of adversities and the world of uncertainties.

The earliest settlers of the island nation of Taiwan are no exception. The annual traditional harvest festival celebrated by Amis, one of the eleven tribes of Taiwan's indigenous inhabitants, is as religious and spiritual as it is social and festive. One of the stories best known among the Amis is the defeat of the spirits called Alikakay after long and hard struggles. "The story I wish to tell you," so it begins,

> is about the Alikakay. The Amis living in the north [of Taiwan] led a happy life. No one exactly knew when Alikakay appeared near them. Since the Alikakay built a small village in Palik near the village of the Amis, misfortunes began to happen to the Amis: babies would die and wives would be violated while their husband were out in the mountains hunting. The Amis decided that to defeat the devious and powerful enemy such as the Alikakay, the different villages ruined by the Alikakay had to unite under one leader. But they were no match for the powerful Alikakay. Frustrated and desperate, they turned to the Kapit, the sea god who taught them a secret to defeat Alikakay. They were to use the *pofog*, a kind of long grass, the leaves of which can be tied in knots and hung in the cover of night on the front door of each Alikakay's house, to exorcise evil spirits. Then they were to hold a sacrificial rite, led by the sorcerers, to worship Heaven, the sea god, and ancestors and to ask them to bless all the Amis. It worked. The Alikakay all became sick and frail. They came to ask for forgiveness. They then walked toward the sea and disappeared. From then on, the Alikakay never appeared again. This is part of the reason why the Amis do various activities in conjunction with the Harvest Festival in September or October.
>
> During the celebration of the Harvest Festival the Amis hold hands, dance and sing, to symbolize the traditionally transmitted sense of belonging to a single ethnic unit. When the sun sets in the west, the young people start to dance around the fire. The burning of the fire represents vitality and the blessing which our ancestors gave us. The main meaning of the ceremony is to call and welcome the spirits of our ancestors to share everything we have. During the festivities the eldest man of the village addresses people of the tribe and welcomes young people who are promoted to join the ranks of leaders. The festival lasts for a week with various activities that involve men, women and young people. It ends as everyone returns to the place of work, wishing each other joy and happiness until the next year when they are together again.[5]

5. Abbreviated and rearranged from chapter 4, "Traditional Harvest Festivals," in Yi et al., *Tracing Origins*, 91–134.

The story is told in a simple manner using ordinary language. But its simple manner and its ordinary language should not make us underestimate the experience of life as dramatic and frightful as that found in the book of Revelation. To put it differently, those of us familiar with the book of Revelation appreciate the drama of life and death told in the Amis story of the life-and-death struggle against the evil spirits of Alikakay.

Just as the life of Christians was endangered by the persecution of the Roman Empire, the life of the Amis was jeopardized by the incursion of the evil spirits called Alikakay. Their efforts to ward off Alikakay proved to be futile. Even after the different villages "united in battle against the Alikakay, they were not able to overcome the destruction created by the Alikakay. They had to resort to the sea god who finally helped them to defeat the evil spirits of the Alikakay.

The Harvest Festival that the Amis hold each year lasts for seven days. Although each day has different activities, the festival is rooted in the history of the people symbolized in the story of the struggle of their ancestors against evil forces. It is the role of the eldest person in the village to tell everyone about their history. In this way the festival brings the community together to remember the past, to renew the communion of tribal people and strengthen their unity as they continue their struggle against the evil powers today, attempting to destroy their tribal solidarity. Renewed and strengthened, they spend the last day of the festival called *Pakelagan*, "gathering with family, friends, and other members of the rank at the seaside or the river bank to relax." After the festival is over, "everyone goes back to the place he or she works, taking good care of oneself until next year. May everyone be merry all year long."[6]

The Harvest Festival observed by the Ami people of Taiwan is not just a merrymaking occasion as the tribal people get together for singing, dancing, drinking and eating. This annual celebration brings them together to share stories of hardships and joys, sorrows and happiness, disappointments and hopes. They also look to the past for inspiration and empowerment and look to the future for hope. It is this essential part of the Harvest Festival that has not been understood by Christians in Taiwan. Even though what the Ami people envision during the Harvest Festival may not be as grand a scale as "the new heaven and the new earth" the Christians to whom the book of Revelation was addressed

6. Ibid., 107.

envisioned, it is as vital to the people of Amis, through the Harvest Festival, to create a new life and tradition out of the life and tradition handed down to them from their remote ancestors.

5. Story Theology in Formation

We have been doing story theology all along, from story itself being a story theology in an embryonic form to storytelling as story theology in practice to story theology as empathetic response to stories and to doing story theology within a renewing community. It is time for us to talk about essential elements that contribute to the formation of story theology.

We live in the universe of meanings. To explore this universe is the task of theology. We cannot emphasize enough our conviction that stories constitute the microcosm of meanings inviting us to explore meanings of the vicissitudes of the life of individuals, families, tribes, and nations on the one hand and, on the other, the macrocosm of meanings summoning us to discover the immense universe of meanings.

This in essence is what story theology is about. It requires something else besides logical reasoning, rational thinking and doctrinal competence, although each of these has its place in the formation of the teachings and doctrines of the church. What is this something else that is essential to story theology? There are a few things that need to be mentioned.

The first thing is *curiosity*. Curiosity is the mother of truths. If you have no curiosity, truths are forever hidden from you. A tree, for instance, is not just a tree. It can mean a whole host of things to artists and to poets. It may tell you secrets in your own heart and mind. It may disclose to you what life, death, and eternal life stand for. It may whisper, say and sing to you the joy and agony of creation.

One recalls what Jesus said. He is exasperated by the lack of curiosity in his listeners, especially the religious authorities, when he prays to God, saying: "I thank you, Father, Lord of heaven and earth, because you have hidden these things from the wise and the intelligent, and have revealed them to infants; yes, Father, for such was your gracious will" (Matt 11:25–26). Note that Jesus addresses God as "Lord of heaven and earth." His God is the Lord of the entire cosmos. To become attuned to whispers, sounds, tones, in them, one has to have curiosity like that of infants and children. No wonder children like stories. In doing story theology we must regain this childlike curiosity!

The second thing is *association*. Story theology has no room for literalism. Is this not why Jesus taught the rule of God in parables? He often begins his message of the rule of God by saying: "To what shall I compare the rule of God?" Jesus compares the rule of God to the mustard seed, to yeast mixed in with flour, treasure hidden in a field, a pearl of unsurpassable value, a net thrown into the sea to catch fish, and so on (Matthew 13). For Jesus the rule of God is not the seed itself, the yeast itself, the treasure itself, the pearl itself, or the net itself. But he is teaching people to associate the rule of God with seed, yeast, treasure, pearl or net, to understand what the rule of God stands for.

The prophet Amos in ancient Judah is a master of association. He gives a very vivid description as if he is "portraying even shadows and sounds" (*hui sheng hui ying* in Chinese) when he says:

> This is what God showed me—a basket of summer fruit.
> God said, "Amos, what do you see?"
> And I said: "A basket of summer fruit."
> Then the Lord said to me,
> "The end has come upon my people Israel:
> I will never again pass them by.
> The songs of the temple shall become
> wailing in that day." (Amos 8:1–3)

The Hebrew word for summer fruit and the word for end sound very similar. Seeing summer fruit, Amos was able to associate it with the end of his nation Israel. He must have shuddered at the sight of summer fruit!

The third thing is *empathy*. What is empathy? It is "the quality and process of entering fully, through imagination, into another's feelings or motives, into the meaning of art, or the like."[7] Empathy is basically a word describing relations of persons. "There is," it is said, "no I as such but only the I of the basic word I-You and the I of the basic word of I-It."[8] The barriers, be they physical, psychological or religious, separating you and other persons, even other things around you, are removed. You live in them and they live in you. Those who are richly endowed with empathy are artists. Without the power of empathy, how can they enter into

---

7. *World Book Dictionary*, 691a.

8. Buber, *I and Thou*, 54.

the life of another person and another thing to become part of them, to perceive meanings in them and to find the resonance of life with them?

Here is a poem composed by a woman poet in ancient China when she discovers that the love that binds her husband and her has waned:

> I take a lump of clay,
> make a figurine of you
> and a figurine of me.
> I crash them together
> to make another figurine of you
> and another figurine of me.
> There is then I in you
> and you in me.[9]

Through this poem the woman poet seeks "to enter into her husband's feelings" in the hope that the love between them may be restored. It describes the closest relations between her and her husband and expresses her deep longing to be one with him again.

This Chinese poem reminds us of the man's exclamation when God introduces to him the woman God has made from him:

> This at last is bone of my bones
> and flesh of my flesh:
> this one shall be called Woman,
> for out of Man this one was taken. (Gen 2:23)

The woman can say the same thing to the man also. The empathy that binds the woman and the man works both ways, enabling them to enter into each other to fathom the meaning of life.

These are perfect examples of how empathy works in artists and in poets. But it should also work in us all who seek to immerse ourselves in a story to be gripped by the passions and insights deeply implanted in it. After all, are we not all artists or poets in one sense or another? Without empathy a story is a story without soul and passion. It remains someone else's story and never becomes my story or your story.

The fourth thing is *imagination*. Imagination is different from fantasy or daydream. The imagination that makes story theology possible is "the power of imagining, of forming pictures in the mind of things not present to the senses." It is "the ability to create new things or ideas or

---

9. The source of this poem, including the name of the woman poet, is lost to me.

to combine old ones in new forms."[10] Not only artists, poets, writers, but even scientists, need this kind of imagination, and those who aspire to story theology need it, a lot of it!

In the creation story in the Hebrew Bible we are told where this power of imagining comes from. It comes from God. This is what we read in Gen 1:27:

> So God created humankind in God's image,
> in the image of God he created them;
> male and female God created them.

Read the word "image" not as a noun but as a verb, then it means "to picture in one's mind, to portray, to symbolize."[11] Our power to image things, to picture something in our mind, to portray them and symbolize them, is our innate ability and power. It is the ability and power God gives us at our birth. Because we are endowed with this God-given power and ability, we are able "to picture in our minds, to portray and to symbolize," that is, to comprehend meanings in a story. The more we possess this power and ability, the more creatively we are able to do story theology.

THE BIBLE, STORIES, AND THEOLOGY

To be able to do story theology, you need to recover these four essential elements of curiosity, association, empathy and imagination. They have been given to you by God; they are innate in you. You must become aware of them in you and recover them. But to do creative story theology, you do not merely become aware of them and recover them, you must sharpen them as you sharpen your tools when you start making things. As these tools of story theology are sharpened with practice, especially through trial and error, you can identify the critical moment (*kairos*) that shapes and fashions a story. *Kairos* is the key to unlock a story, to unravel its structure, enabling you to come to grips with its meanings. These critical moments (*kairoi*) make the stories in the Bible and other stories reflect one another and interact one with another, helping us come to grips with different levels of theological meanings in the story. Since there are often stories within a story, as we discussed in chapter 7, there can be more than one *kairos* in a story. One *kairos* or many *kairoi*,

10. *World Book Dictionary*, 1054a.
11. Ibid., 1053c.

it is essential that the *kairos* or *kairoi* are identified, for they provide clues to the understanding and interpretation of the story.

Let us recall some of the stories to which we have referred in the previous chapters. Take the story of Abraham offering Isaac as a sacrifice to God. The moment Abraham raises the knife to kill his son Isaac is one of the *kairoi* in the story. Isaac asking his father where the sheep for sacrifice is another. Abraham hearing the voice saying to him not to kill Isaac is another. Sarah sensing something wrong between the father and the son is yet another. All these *kairoi* deepen and at the same time broaden our understanding of the story, leading to quite the contrary conclusion that the story is about Abraham testing God and not God testing Abraham.

Hans Christian Anderson's "The Ugly Duckling" also comes to mind. There is also more than one *kairos* in the story—the *kairos* of the large and hard egg finally cracked open to begin the miserable life of "the duckling," the *kairos* of the "duckling" finally deciding to leave the miserable life at home to venture out into an unknown world, and the *kairos* of "the duckling" seeing its own reflection of a beautiful swan in the lake.

What about Mary's Magnificat? If the Magnifcat is perceived as a song of praise summing up Mary's life and not as simply celebrating her conception of Jesus, we may discern several *kairoi* in it: the *kairos* of her perception that the Spirit is instrumental in her conception, the *kairos* of her realization that God is the God of the oppressed, the *kairos* of her awareness that Jesus is destined to serve the rule of God, and the *kairos* of the decision of her faith in the resurrection through the suffering and death of her son Jesus on the cross. These *kairoi* of the Magnificat are like a prism reflecting various dimensions of faith—not only of Mary's but ours also—faith in the suffering and redeeming God through Jesus.

Just as stories in the Bible consist of many decisive moments that invite us to explore messages at much deeper levels, so do many stories outside the Bible. Each decisive moment, whether biblical or otherwise, is special and different, but these special and different decisive moments could also be mutually resonant and vibrational, enabling us to find ourselves in the presence of the *meaning* that illumines our search for an eternal life in the temporal world. Theology grows out of these decisive moments, resonating and vibrating with them. Hence, stories are the main sources of theology, and that theology informed by stories—immersing in them, and resting with them, stories of faith, hope and love—is what we call *story theology*.

Bibliography

Alighieri, Dante. *The Inferno: Dante's Immortal Drama of a Journey through Hell.* Translated by John Ciardi. New York: Signet, 1954.

Augustine. *The City of God.* Translated by Marcus Dodd. New York: Modern Library, 1950.

———. *Confessions.* Translated with introduction by R. S. Pine-Coffin. New York: Penguin, 1961.

Barton, John, and John Muddiman. *The Oxford Bible Commentary.* Oxford: Oxford University Press, 2001.

Battenhouse, Roy W., editor. *A Companion to the Study of St. Augustine.* New York: Oxford University Press, 1955.

Brown, Peter. *Augustine of Hippo: A Biography.* 1st ed. Berkeley: University of California Press, 1967.

Buber, Martin. *I and Thou.* Translated by Walter Kaufmann. New York: Touchstone, 1996.

Buttrick, George Arthur, editor. *The Interpreter's Dictionary of the Bible.* 4 vols. Nashville: Abingdon, 1962.

Chan, Wing-Tsit, translator. *A Source Book in Chinese Philosophy.* Princeton: Princeton University Press, 1963.

Chang, Iris. *The Rape of Nanking.* New York: Penguin, 1997.

Cole, Joanna, editor. *Best-Loved Folktales of the World.* New York: Anchor, 1983.

Collins English Dictionary. 3rd ed. Glasgow: HarperCollins, 1991.

Conze, Edward, translator. *Buddhist Scriptures.* Penguin, 1959.

Dao-Sheng, Lin, editor. *Collection of Myths and Stories of Aborigines.* Taipei: Han Yi Se Yen Wen Hua Enterprise, 2002.

De Bary, William Theodore. *The Buddhist Tradition in India, China and Japan.* New York: Random House, 1972.

Dorson, Richard M. *Folk Legends of Japan.* Vermont: Charles E. Tuttle, 1962.

———, editor. *Folktales Told around the World.* Chicago: University of Chicago Press, 1975.

Eliade, Mircea. *From Primitives to Zen: A Thematic Sourcebook of the History of Religions.* London: Williams Collins, 1967.

———. *Images and Symbols.* Princeton: Princeton University Press, 1991.

Elwell, Walter A., editor. *Evangelical Dictionary of Theology.* Grand Rapids: Baker, 1984.

Figgis, J. N. *The Political Aspects of St. Augustine's City of God.* London: 1921.

Fischer, Louis. *The Life of Mahatma Gandhi.* San Francisco: Harper & Row, 1950.

Green, Martin. *Gandhi in India, In His Own Words.* Hanover, NH: University Press of New England, 1987.

Haley, Alex. *Roots.* London: Pan, 1977

Keigwin, R. P., translator. *Hans Christian Anderson: Eighty Fairy Tales.* New York: Pantheon, 1982.

The Learning Bible. Contemporary English Version. New York: American Bible Society, 2000.

Leeming, David. *A Dictionary of Asian Mythology.* New York: Oxford University Press, 2001.

Legges, James, translator. *The Chinese Classics.* Hong Kong: Hong Kong University Press, 1960.

Mardrus, J. C., and Powys Mathers. *The Book of the Thousand Nights and One Night.* 2nd ed. Yugoslavia: Droset, 1987.

McGrath, Alister E., editor. *The Christian Theology Reader.* Oxford: Blackwell, 1995.

Miles, Margaret R. *The Word Made Flesh: A History of Christian Thought.* Oxford: Blackwell, 2005.

Mintz, Alan. "Introduction." In *A Treasury of Jewish Folklore,* edited by Nathan Ausubel. New York: Bantam, 1980.

The New American Desk Encyclopedia. 3rd ed. New York: Penguin, 1984.

Nishio, Kanji. *New History Textbook.* Tokyo: Fuso, 2001.

Songs of the Pacific. In *Risk,* vol. 12, no. 1. Geneva: World Council of Churches, 1976.

Soothhill, William Edward, and Lewis Hodus, compilers. *A Dictionary of Chinese Buddhist Terms.* Delhi: Motilal Banarsidass, 1977.

Vanhoozer, Kevin J. "Evangelicalism and the Church: The Company of the Gospel." In *Futures of Evangelicalism: Issues and Prospects,* edited by Craig Bartholomew, Robin Parry, and Andrew West, 40–99. Leicester: InterVarsity, 2003.

Webster's New World Dictionary. 3rd college ed. New York: Simon & Schuster, 1994.

Westermann, Claus. *Genesis 1–11: A Commentary.* Translated by John J. Scullion. Minneapolis: Augsburg, 1987.

———. *Genesis 12–36: A Commentary.* Translated by John J. Scullion. Minneapolis: Augsburg, 1981.

Wiesel, Elie. *The Gates of the Forest.* New York: Avon, 1966.

———. *Night.* New York: Bantam, 1960.

———. *One Generation After.* New York: Schocken, 1982.

The World Book Dictionary. Chicago: World Book, 1984.

The World Book Encyclopedia. Volume A. Chicago: World Book, 1982.

Wu Ming, Yi et al. *Tracing Origins: Customs and Festivals of Amis on the East Coast of Taiwan.* Taipei: Tourism Department, Ministry of Transportation, 1992.

Zipes, Jack, editor. *Aesop's Fables.* London: Penguin, 1996.